Engithidong Xugixudhoy

Their Stories of Long Ago

Engithidong Xugixudhoy

Their Stories of Long Ago

Told in Deg Hit'an Athabaskan
by Belle Deacon of Anvik

Recorded by Karen McPherson and James Kari

Transcribed and edited by James Kari

Translated by Belle Deacon and James Kari
with the help of
Jim Dementi, Grace John, Alta Jerue, Chad Thompson,
Donna MacAlpine, and Eliza Jones

Illustrated by Cindy Davis

Foreword by Donna MacAlpine

Preface by James Kari

Alaska Native Language Center
College of Liberal Arts, University of Alaska
Fairbanks

and

Iditarod Area School District
McGrath

1987

Engithidong Xugixudhoy
Their Stories of Long Ago

Printed in the United States of America

Library of Congress Cataloging in Publication Data
Deacon, Belle, 1905–
Engithidong Xugixudhoy: their stories of long ago/told in Deg Hit'an Athabaskan by Belle Deacon; recorded by Karen McPherson and James Kari; transcribed and edited by James Kari; translated by Belle Deacon and James Kari with the help of Jim Dementi... [et al.]; illustrated by Cindy Davis; foreword by Donna MacAlpine; preface by James Kari.
p. cm.
ISBN 1-55500-031-2 (pbk.)
1. Ingalik Indians—Legends. 2. Indians of North America—Alaska—Legends. 3. Ingalik language—Texts. I. McPherson, Karen. II. Kari, James M. III. Alaska Native Language Center. IV. Iditarod Area School District (McGrath, Alaska) V. Title.
E99.I5D43 1987 87-33321
398.2'08997—dc 19 CIP

First printing 1987 500 copies

Address correspondence to: Alaska Native Language Center
Box 900111
University of Alaska
Fairbanks, AK 99775-0120

Contents

Foreword vii
Preface ix

The Stories

Deg Hit'an Gixudhoy
'The People's Stories' 2

Niłoqay Ni'idaxin
'The Man and Wife' 5
The Old Man Who Came Down from Above the Second Layer of This World 34

Taxghozr
'Polar Bear' 41
Polar Bear 58

Niq'odałin Notin Nixidaxin
'The Two Girls Who Lived There' 61
Two Girls and Crow Man 78

Niłeda Sugiluqye Yixo Dixodałdiyh
'Two Cousins Shooting Arrows' 83

Tr'an Sughiluq Tthux Ni'idhit
'The Old Woman Who Lived Alone' 91
The Old Lady Who Lived Alone 104

Nołdith Gixudhoy
'Hawk Owl Story' 107

Q'ivałdal Tixgedr Yił
'Spruce Grouse and Mink' 111
Spruce Grouse and Mink 118

Tr'an Sughiluq Chighiligguy Gho'in Xididhitl'ighanh
'The Old Woman Who Killed Herself Because of the Fox' 121

Foreword

Some of Belle's family at winter camp at Miyok Slough on the Anvik River in April, early 1930s. From left: Belle Deacon; Dolly, Belle's daughter; Jean Young, Lucius Young's first wife; Lucius Young, Belle's brother; Julia Young, Belle's stepmother; John Young, Belle's father; and Jimmy Young, Belle's brother. Photo from the Belle Deacon collection.

It is good to have traditional stories on paper, written down so that future generations may read the words of their elders long after the storytellers are gone. When I think of traditional stories, however, I think of listening to Belle Deacon, of her voice and expression, of the rhythm and cadence that make the stories come alive. Whether the story is in English or in Belle's native Deg Hit'an, you feel as if you can almost follow what is happening without the words. Whether in a crowded room at a big city museum or sitting quietly at the kitchen table with a late-night cup of tea, Belle can fascinate you and hold you spellbound with the power of her voice as she relates the old, old tales handed down by generations of her people.

Belle was born in the fall of 1905 as her family was traveling up the Yukon River from Anvik. They stopped by the bluffs below where the village of Grayling has since been built, and there she was born. Her father was John Young, originally from the Innoko River, and her mother was Ellen, daughter of one of the chiefs of Anvik. Her parents already had one daughter, and her mother had lost several children. In the years that followed, another daughter and two sons were born. Belle now is the last of her family.

In the early days the family spent most of their year up the Anvik River at the mouth of the Yellow River, coming down the river each spring soon after the ice went out. One year, when Belle was 14, her family left her at Anvik Mission in the fall to receive her first formal schooling. In her earliest memories of Anvik, there were a few people still living on Anvik Point, but most of the houses were up on the Anvik River where it made its last bend before coming down to the Yukon. She remembers all the houses there and who lived in each, and she has helped schoolchildren draw a map of that village where now there are only depressions in the tall grass and willows.

Belle's grandmother Marcia, her mother's mother, lived with the family while Belle was growing up. As Belle explains it, her grandmother was a rich woman in the Indian way, having everything she needed, until her husband died in 1900. Then she had to do handwork for people, sewing and making baskets, for which people gave her a little fish or whatever they had as payment. As Marcia worked, Belle would sit by her and watch, listening to the stories her grandmother told of Anvik and of the ways of her people.

When Marcia was young, she was known as a very powerful woman. She was big and tough and, according to Belle, could pack a big tree by herself, or lick three men. On one occasion, she even broke a beaver hip bone by twisting it in her hands when none of the men in the kashim were able to do it. She also for a time had special spiritual powers, but her father kept her from being a shaman because he feared for her safety. She was the only child he had left out of fifteen children, and he did not want to lose her.

Belle's grandmother Marcia laces snowshoes as Belle looks on. Photo from the Belle Deacon Collection.

As a child, Belle was favored by Marcia and was taught how to live a good and long life, never to swear, and always to be kind and help the old people. Marcia foretold that Belle would outlive the rest of her family, so it was to Belle that she passed on the traditional skills and knowledge she possessed. By watching Marcia work, and then by trying it herself, Belle learned the craftsmanship which has made her well-known in Alaska for her birchbark baskets. And as she watched and listened, she also learned the stories—tales of her grandmother's life, the history of Anvik "from story beginning," and traditional stories of her people. In addition, Belle learned many of the old stories from elders who came to her family during hard times. These elders did not tell their stories to just anyone, but they would relate them to Belle's family in gratitude for the food they received. Marcia, her daughter Ellen, and many Anvik elders died in 1927 in the flu epidemic that wiped out much of the population in the Anvik area.

Belle was married twice, first to Henry Gochenauer, a trader from upriver, and then, after he died, to John Deacon of Holikachuk. John died in 1985 at the age of 96. Belle raised two families, supporting her children after she was first widowed by trapping on her own, and later by doing handwork as her grandmother had done. Now 83, Belle has spent a lot of time in the last ten years demonstrating her basket-making skills and telling stories to groups of people all over Alaska. She has also made several trips to Anvik to talk to the school children there, and to tell them about the history of their village and the people who used to live there.

This collection of stories is only a small part of the treasure which Belle possesses, and we are grateful that she has taken the time to do the recording, listening, and proofing required to put traditional stories into written form. Through this book these stories are coming to new generations from Grandmother Marcia and from other elders of Anvik, going back into the distant time.

DONNA MACALPINE — Iditarod Area School District, June 1987

Preface

The Athabaskan people of the lower-middle Yukon River region, in the villages of Anvik, Shageluk, and Holy Cross, and of the middle Kuskokwim River region, in the vicinity of Stony River village, have been referred to in published sources as "Ingalik." These people call themselves Deg Hit'an 'the local people', and in recent years their language has been designated by this name.

Belle has participated in shows sponsored by the Institute of Alaska Native Arts and the University of Alaska Museum highlighting the works of Native artists. (Photo by Rose Atuk Fosdick from Interwoven Expressions, *courtesy of the Institute of Alaska Native Arts.)*

Belle Deacon is one of the foremost Deg Hit'an storytellers of her generation. Typically, Belle tells these stories in her living room while she works on the birchbark and willow root baskets for which she is widely known. Her late husband, John Deacon, who spoke Holikachuk rather than Deg Hit'an, often served as her audience. John would listen carefully and offer an occasional comment or chuckle. It was fascinating to hear them conversing in two distinct Athabaskan languages.

The stories are presented here in a facing-page format with the Deg Hit'an on the left and the English on the right. We have attempted to make the English translation flow smoothly while retaining the essence of the Deg Hit'an, not always an easy task given the differences between the languages. We have also included Belle's English versions of five of the stories. These have been edited to remove false starts and ambiguities, and editorial insertions have occasionally been made for clarity, but the stories are printed largely as Belle told them. Italic type in these stories (*e.g., big*) indicates emphasis; capital letters (*e.g.,* BIG) indicate an increase in volume. Words with three hyphens (*e.g.,* bi---g) indicate that Belle drew out the word as she said it.

Most of the stories in this book were recorded in 1973 by Karen McPherson, then of the Alaska State Library's Alaska Native Oral Literature Project. James Kari of the Alaska Native Language Center, University of Alaska, recorded some of the stories in 1981 and 1985. The stories presented here represent about forty percent of the collection that Belle Deacon has recorded to date. Other untranscribed stories tell of

Anvik area history and geography.

The stories were transcribed in Deg Hit'an by James Kari and were translated primarily by Belle Deacon and Kari, with help in proofreading and translation from the late John Deacon, the late Bertha Dutchman, Jim Dementi, Alta Jerue, Grace John, and Hannah Maillelle. Chad Thompson, Eliza Jones, Jane McGary, and Irene Reed of the Alaska Native Language Center and Donna MacAlpine of the Iditarod Area School District also assisted with proofreading and translations. Jane McGary and Shari Sirkin typed earlier drafts of the stories. Lorraine Basnar Elder typeset the book and offered many editorial suggestions.

The late John Deacon, left, helps Belle prepare materials for her baskets. (Photo by Tom Sadowski, courtesy of University of Alaska Museum.)

We acknowledge with thanks the Alaska State Library for support of McPherson's work in 1973; the National Science Foundation for support of Kari's Deg Hit'an language work in 1976-78 (grant no. BNS-76-18647); and the Iditarod Area School District's bilingual-bicultural program for support of work by Kari, Thompson, and MacAlpine from 1980 to 1987.

JAMES KARI — Alaska Native Language Center, August 1987

The Stories

Deg Hit'an Gixudhoy

Yitots'in' sigixudhoy ditil'iyo ts'in' xughun' dixin'ne.
Engthi dong xodhił xits'in':
"Xełedz yi viłnuxłting ts'in' xełedz uxłchik iy yidong xinag"
dinadidene' sraqay itlanh dong.
"Yitots'in' vił axa duxt'a' ne' vił q'ixudinuxdiyił.
Yitots'in ghitidhuxtinogts'in'.
Yixudz vighoyen'uxdhił.
Agide yidong xinag yitołchiłdi dina'ididine' yidong."
Axaxiłdik vighun' xuyo ditr'ił'anh xuyozr n'a,
"Dinats'in' xuxłdhoyh," dina'ididine tux.
Tr'ixutiłdhoyh tux dinanotthi yoqoyh ghidiq'uk hiq'i
dinitl'idik hiq'i ts'in' tr'ihohał ts'in' hiq'idingit'a.

The People's Stories

They said this about the way my stories go.
In the time of long ago [they would tell us this]:
"If you don't fall asleep, you can obtain the old wisdom"
that was being told to us when I was a child.
"Even if you are sleepy, you should try to stay awake.
And you shouldn't fidget.
You should just think about everything.
Then you'll get the old wisdom that was told to us in the past."
After we'd thought about it a little,
"Tell it to us," they would say to us.
When we start to tell it, [a story] is like a bright light ahead of us,
just as though it were written as we speak.

Niłʼoqay Niʼidaxin
The Man and Wife

"This story came from Anvik when I was around maybe twelve years old... One named Old Jackson told this story to four of us girls. And he told us to listen to it good, because if you don't get the stories [now], even if you never even think about it [again], you don't [ever] get the story. He told us to really think about it. It comes from way [back] generation[s], from the story beginning. They pass it on to one another. That's what he told us."

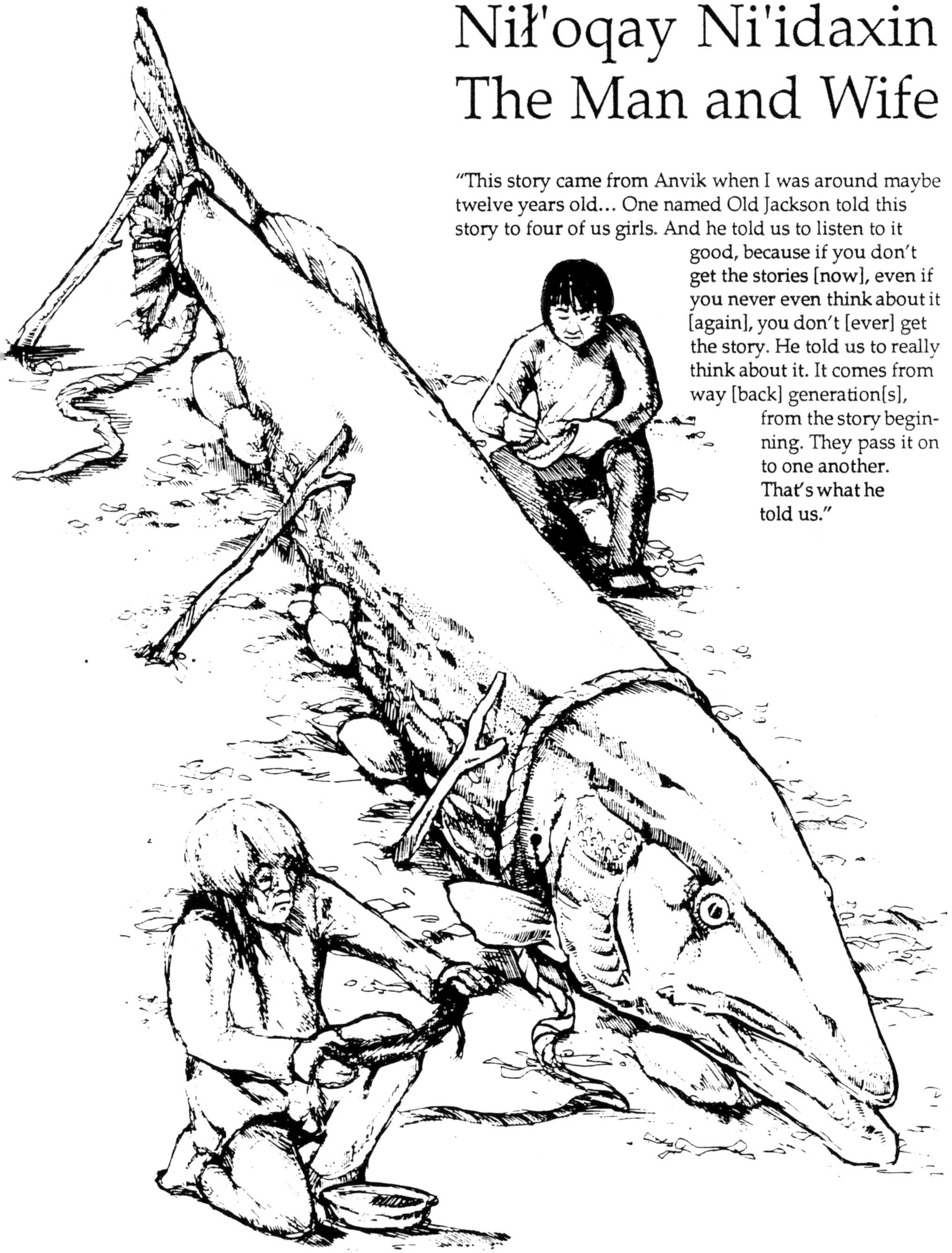

Niłoqay Ni'idaxin

Niłoqay tr'in'ne deg nixidax srixno' xudo'.
Ts'an yixi xathdo nixudodhil ts'in'.
Yiy getiy hits'i tr'ixine'ots xiyił xantr'ixixuneg.
Ndagh sre' hits'in' xivixelanh ło go.

Ts'an yitots'in' getiy xiyts'in' nonxudidhik hiłdi nonxałdilayh.
Yixudz xał getiy long diłan,
xałts'in' tux ni'edoyh deg vighothq'idz yixudz xiyił gitsighiy axa.
Emedz dixet'a hingo che vixal dhidh che didindiggit ło go.
Ts'an yitongo vi'ot hiłdi ngi'egh q'u'idiniyh.
Ngi'egh hiłdi q'u'idiniyh ts'in' yixudz tritr yił hits'in' din'ilyayh.
Ngi'ot hidoy yixudz higidanełdzaq.
Hingo chenh xiyenqun'dilayh xałts'in' tux.
Yixudz hiłdik q'u'alniyh hiłdi nilodiłanh.
Di'ak neg yił yi'eghoyh giqałchin yił, gisr yił, ts'ix yił, ts'id yił,
ixutiy yił di'egh yixudz giggiddh nołchidl yet nonyidiniggit.
Giggiddh nołchidl chux ndadz dighontitl'ichogh chux.
Dighondiniggit.
Axaxiłdik tso q'idz donyalyayh.
Diqing' hiłdik nughuł didithne'its'in'.
Viqing' ni'idoyh dihiłdik tth'ax yan' gide xiniditth.
"Gan dangłan'?" yidithne' ts'in' ts'ixuyił.
Ts'an yixudz ye getiy sidałts'eyh.
Axaxiłdi yoxo xiyił giłvatr.
Xotłogh tux hiłdik, "Ey gil vanhgiq, ey vanhgiq yan' getiy q'at.
Che vixighigi'an' yi giq'ux vanhgiq hey," [yiłne].
Ts'an giq'ux vanhgiq yighun ni'iqoyh ts'ixuyan'.
Iy hiłdi ihonh xotl'ogh hiłdi gighontthe'iłch'ił ts'ixuyił.
Iy gitsighiy gan inałt'ay ghuntthitr'iłch'ił viluxdong' che yit dhidlo.
Getiy long ts'in'.
Vinixułts'eg yoqoyh davo tr'i'idhik.
Yiluxdong' che ghontthe'iłch'ił.
Yiye gilayh ngi'egh doyighidelayh ts'in'.

The Man and Wife[1]

A man and wife, they say, lived at the mouth of a side stream.
They lived there year in and year out.
They didn't know how they got there.
They didn't know where they came from.

One time, when it was becoming fall, [the man] put traps out.
He did a lot of trapping,
and every evening he came back with marten piled over his shoulders.
His pack was completely stuffed full of skins, too.
His wife worked outdoors.
As she worked outdoors, she made a big pile of firewood.
She had all the wood piled up by the door.
She also built a fire every evening.
Having finished all that work, she sewed.
She made beautiful parkas, boots, mittens, caps, and blankets,
which she packed away in big storage bags.
What great big storage bags they were, so big.
She filled them up.
Then she put them in the cache.
She never told her husband what she was doing.
Whenever her husband came home, she would just be twisting thread..
He never asked her, "What are you doing?"
This made her very happy.
She cooked for him.
After that, always, "I really want some ice cream, that's all.
I'm so accustomed to that fat ice cream," he said.
So she always took the ice cream to him.
After he ate that, then he skinned what he trapped.
He skinned all the marten and he left some in a big pile there.
There were many of them.
Early in the morning, before dawn, he would wake up.
He would skin the rest.
He put them on stretchers and hung them up outside.

1. When Belle tells this story in English, she calls it "The Old Man Who Came Down from Above the Second Layer of This World." See p. 34.

Xotl'ogh hiłdi che gits'i'in ntidoyh.
"Dingt'a q'idighutux dran dhedhig ts'in' ts'an,
vaxa ndadz ditet'el gan inałt'ay gidhidh dingł'an?" yiłne.
"Dixulingith ts'in' dran tasdhił?"di'adidene hingo.
"Yixudz getiy tr'inay axa ts'an'a dist'a yixudz."
"Xik'o xidinigitoyh ts'an'a gide xidist'anh," yiłne.
"A, gil tr'a'ine," yiłne.

Ts'an yitots'in' hiłdik ntidoyh.
Ntidoyh hingo hiłdi niłts'e'idangiditl'eyh,
didhidh axa xiyił xin'ałchith.
Niq'ołonh yozr yixudz yeg viggaghidithitth'iq hiq'i hanh ts'il anh.
Dina'ideloy getiy dezren ye'ithitl'enh.
Niq'ołonh xuyozr xit'a che ngizrenh.
Yixudz yeg dina' hiq'i hanh.
I'ey got yoxo denendhinh viqing';
ni'idoyh hiłdi ditsisdogga' q'idiyitldo ts'ixuyan' yołtał ts'in'.
Nnn ts'an yixudz deł'anh xotl'ogh nigixidonh, hiłdi xintayh.

Yitongo hiłdi gidegh nitidoyh tux ginot yił nintth'ix.
Q'idughutux che che yith vanhgiq nintth'ix.
Gan yixudz ditthig genavadr yił getiy xełedz gixihonh.
Ts'an dixunałt'adi sre' nixudodhił yixudz dixit'anh,
dał idivenhditux nigintth'ix ts'ixuyan'.
Ng'ot hiłdi ttheting heyitlqonh ithitinh.
Sanhtux xizro yiggi xiyitohel adhin yozr nintth'ix
dixo'in tiłjit yinedhin ts'in'.

Axaxiłdik xiyts'in' nonxudidhit.
Idighił nixuthiq'otth che che chenh nonxałnelo.
I---y.
Ixuxuyił yixudz ndadz sre' didiyoq vaxa antr'a' gits'i hiq'i.
Antr'a yixudz yit
"Gaq'a viyan' ts'igo nghiniginistth'ix ts'in' ts'ihiq'i di'ist'i' ts'in'," inedhinh.
"Gełuxdi yadi nadhoł vanhgiq ndadz ditoneł?" inedhinh.
Ts'an yitots'in' axaxiłdik xałts'in' nixunedhit digił'anh ts'in'
ngi'o hiłdi tritr yił di'ił'el ts'in' yixudz vaxa antr'a gits'i idingit'a.
Axaxiłdik, xałts'in' ni'idiyo.
Ngidugg xiyegighe'onh iy yighun' iłchet.
Axaxiłdik dhivadr yighonineqonh,
go eyiggi din'ne ts'in', yit nonxudidhit xuyił,

After that he'd go hunting again.
"Why don't you stay home a day sometimes;
what will you do with all those skins you're getting, anyway?" she said to him.
"How many days will I be alone?" she asked him.
"I get very lonesome here."
"I do it because I enjoy being out," he said.
"Ah, keep yourself busy," he said to her.

Soon after that, he left again.
As soon as he left, she started sewing again,
putting her belt around her waist.
This young woman was just very neat, very clean and orderly.
She was dressed in very pretty clothes.
The young woman was very pretty.
She was just like a doll.
And her husband thought a lot of her;
whenever he came home, he always put her on his knees, holding her.
After he did that, they would eat and then go to bed.

Whenever he went out, she would make him fish ice cream.
Once in a while, too, she would make snow ice cream.
With all that, and the half-dried fish, they had plenty to eat.
I don't know how many years went by while they went on this way,
doing the same things every day, nothing else.
They would leave the ice cream outside to keep it cool.
In the summer, when it was not very cool outside, she made only enough ice cream for one meal
because she didn't want it to get sour.

Fall came again.
Soon it got cold again, and he started setting traps again.
I---y.
One day, I don't know what happened, but she didn't feel well.
And so then
"I don't feel like making ice cream," she thought.
"If he goes one night without ice cream, what will happen?" she thought to herself.
Soon evening fell as she was sewing,
and she didn't get any firewood because she just didn't feel well.
In the evening he came back.
He lowered his pack and she took it.
Then she gave him what was cooked,
and, when the time came,

"Xidiy iy vanhgiq?" yiłne.
"Ngo, vanhgiq ninistth'igh ts'in'.
Saxa gits'in' xiq'its'in' dran ghisdhił yixudz, yiq'idist'a ts'ixuyił xik'o ts'idz dist'a *all day*," yiłne.
"No, I couldn't."
"Vaxa getiy viq'at iy dałine', ethe niginatth'aq ts'i'a ngo,
gitidhasel ts'in' xiq'i dist'a.
Eyighod getiy an'a getiy xełedz gisonh ts'i yixudz tthidan'isidhik," yiłne.

Axaxiłdik "Diyo ixan vanhgiq yozr ngoxo dhitltse'?" yiłne.
"Isre' lingith," yiłne.
Ts'an ng'in tthitadhiyo.
Tingił yozr iłchet tigith'o yiggi che iłchet.
Ngi'in yitots'in' ngo yith oqo.
"Yith nagh ni'enastth'ix," yiłne.
Ngi'in tthitadhiyo ts'in' tthidi vadi xutadhit.
Yiggi xidontodolinh ghile chenh.
Vadi xutidhi'o'.
Xidigał yixudz xiyodititl-'an'.
"Xidanh si'ot, ndadz didiyoq?
Q'ode dingt'a tthitihoyh tux ghilechenh
q'agh xidon'idoyh," yinedhinh.
Axaxiłdik yixudz giyenghit'atth ts'in' yixudz ngi'in yiq'igheyo.
Ts'an yitots'in' ng'in yoqo tthitadhiyo.
Ng'egh yoqo xinayh ine' xida' anh xidanh?
Ngidixi tso yet xuyił yoqo xiniłanh.
Giq'idixidetth'iq.
Nnn, viqul.
Axaxiłdik xidon'idiyo ts'in hiłdik q'eyh iqun'dinłtthiyh.
Iy axa ngi'egh yix xanot dhiyo dina ting hiqul ts'ixuyił.
Ngitthing tthatadhiyo xuyił yiggiy tingił.
Ngitthing xizro lo che ting dhitonhdi.
Iy ghotthing che che tigitth'o yiggiy dhitonh.
Tiginq'at xuyan' xuts'in' dina ting xelanh yixo'egh xuyił dina ting qul.
"Iiy ndadz didiyogginh?" yinedhinh.
"Ndadz sre' didiyoq ts'igo?" inedhinh.
Xidon'idiyo ts'in' yixudz tathtrax.
"Sigho'in'a didiyoq.
Gan layinh chenh niginetth'ix vidisnenh?
Dingit'a gełixi vadi tthididhitldhed che ts'ighitl-'o'," inedhinh.
Ts'an axaxiłdik tathtrax yixi nithitrax yixudz.
Venhdi vinixułts'eg che ngi'egh che q'ontithiyo yoqo nixolyax ts'in'.

"Where is the ice cream?" he said to her.
"Well, I didn't make ice cream.
I haven't felt well
all day," she said.
"No, I couldn't [make it]."
"Well, I really want it; you should still make it;
I won't get full [without it].
Whenever I eat that, I sleep well all night," he told her.

"Well, why don't I make a little ice cream for you?" she said to him.
"If you want to," he told her.
So she went outside.
She took a little bowl and she took a wooden spoon too.
Then she went outside for snow.
"I'll make it with snow," she said to him.
She went outside and was gone a long time.
She never came back in.
She was gone a long time.
Finally, he started worrying about her.
"Where is my wife, what's happened to her?
It isn't like her to be gone so long; when she goes out,
she usually comes right back," he thought.
Then he put on his boots and went out after her.
He went out to search for her.
He called for her, but where was she?
He looked for her up in the cache.
It was quiet.
She wasn't there.
Then he went into the house and lit a piece of birch bark.
He walked around outside with it, but he could not find any tracks.
Then he went down the path, and there was her bowl.
There it was, lying beside the trail.
Farther down [the trail] lay the wooden spoon.
The tracks went only as far as the water hole, and there were no other tracks around.
"Iiy, what has happened to her?" he thought.
"What could have happened?" he thought.
He went back in and started crying.
"It's all my fault.
Why did I ever tell her to make ice cream?
I should have gone without it," he thought.
He started crying and he just kept on crying.
Early the next morning he went out again, searching for her.

Ine' dina ting xuyił xuqul.
Xał dathdlo xixits'idz xuyił ideyan' viting xelanh.
Xits'idz yixo'egh tritr dił'anh dixuyan' vi'o ting helanh.
Edi yixudz xidiqay xanot dina ting xoqo q'ith
ine' viyan' dina ting xuqul.
Ixuxuyił ghilegot axaxiłdi xidon'idiyo.
Axaxiłdi tathtrax.
Dran nigiditrix.
Githon ts'in'.
Ts'ixuyił dadz yixudz ye ge tth'inh yił natidhighił
ine' idiq'itl'ineg ts'in' xuyił.
Getiy yiggi tho'idiniyh xiyozr yiggi genoggoddh k'idz yozr
axa didrogg getiy detseyh tux etle'.
Go deg dilo' nił'anh tux yixudz vilo' tth'in zro.
Yixudz yeg dinaqgg xuyił ditalniyh.
Dinaqogg ndadz ditalniyh tux go vanhtl'otthing' tth'in zro tr'ixudidhi'o.
"Inagh dighut'a'," inedhinh.
"Se deyan' sigho'in in'a vixedhinix," inedhinh.
"Inagh got istrix ts'in' go go yix yixudz sitth'in noghidałdi.
Go yit sidinegginghdi.
It will be fine," inedhinh.
"Se n'at sigho'in ixudz didiyoq," inedhinh.
Ts'an xidigał, xizro lo che yixudz ngi'in yiggi tritr k'idz
vi'ot diyighił'an oqo tthantidoyh.
Ts'ixuyił xighotiyh denadhit.
Yixudz tiyh adinh dredi tthan'idi'itlniyh.
Ngiyix hiłdi didichonh gidinghiłtl'ith.
Iy axa hiłdi deg xin'ałchith yixudz divit q'angididitth ts'in'.
Tthandititlniyh yixudz tth'inh zro.

Deg xiydi xeyts'in' got didiyoq.
Xiyh tth'ixunedr xits'ixodhił q'idixet'a.
Xizro lo chenh ngi'in ghiłghatl yił.
Ngi'in xits'in' xizro lo chenh dinaqa' nitr'atitlghitl.
Yixudz yiggi imik'i ndadz didiyoq.
"Si'ot ni'idiyo xut'al," inedhinh.
Yit yixudz xineghaldhit xizro lo che viyetr yił yixudz dred xuyił giłtr'eth getiy.
"Ndadz divasre' adit'an?" inedhinh ts'in'.
"Xiday got sitth'in natidhighiłdi divasre' dit'anh?" inedhinh.

But there were no tracks anywhere.
Where he had his traps there were only his own tracks.
Out where she gathered wood were only her own tracks.
He searched all around the village for human tracks,
but there were no others.
He went inside.
He started to cry.
He cried all day.
He didn't eat.
He started getting thin
without realizing it.
He would eat a tiny bit, a little dried fish
for the chest pains when he became very hungry.
When he looked down at his fingers, they were all bony.
He felt his body with his hands.
When he felt his face with his hands, his cheekbones felt as if they were protruding.
"That's fine," he thought.
"Because of me, she's gone," he thought.
"So it must be that [I'm destined to] cry in this house and my bones will drop here.
I'll starve to death here.
It will be fine," he thought.
"What happened to her was my fault," he thought.
Finally, he went outside to get a little of the wood
that his wife had stacked by the door.
His strength was failing.
He was so weak, he could barely go outside.
He bound something around his belly.[2]
He tied it around his stomach and bound up his clothes.
He went outside; he was getting so thin.

All fall this happened.
Then it came to be mid-winter.
It had become dark outside.
Outside the door there came the sound of someone knocking the snow off his boots.
The man just did not know what to do.
"Maybe my wife came back," he thought.
He stayed still there, barely breathing.
"Who could it be?" he was thinking.
"Who could it be at this place where my bones are about to drop?" he thought.

2. Belle says that this was done in times of starvation. He was so skinny that his clothes were loose and he needed binding to keep them on him.

Axaxiłdik ixuxuyił xizro lo chenh yadz gititl'inek.
Diva zro lo chenh?
Dina tiyh sughiluq xizro lo chenh,
dina tiyh ts'il q'ul yozr anh xizro lo chenh ng'o xidineyodi.
"Ne---," yiłne.
"Dina ło xelanh," yiłne.
"Sitthey," yiłne.
"Go nginqogg xiyet nigenisitoyh tux
ngiq'anginisitoyh tux getiy k'on'ne di'idene ts'in'.
Sitl'o xiyet n'at yixudz iłt'e ngitrix.
Yitots'in' ngitth'in yił natoghułdi xits'i xodhił ts'an go dist'anh.
Giyen oxo dadz ditidhasnel ts'in', ine' xiłdik getiy ngo denisdhinh.
Getiy xełedz xuneg donłuxli'an' ngi'ot nghu ixedhinix.
Xits'in' nggot dadz disiyoq.
Ngo sitl'o xiyet in'a ixudz didene," yiłne.

"Gila'?" yiłne.
"Gil dixughit'a' ts'i didene;
agide ngo xantidhaginigh ts'in' ts'an'at ixudzdidene," yiłne.
Axaxiłdi yixudz niłts'i idan-giditl'enh ts'i xiłdi tthitadhiyo.

Gan xizro lo chenh yixudz ghinoth viye niłighilighalinh.
Gitsighith ts'id
yił viye itlchedh yitongo che giłts'ay yath ts'id iche che yałts'idz didighonh.
Xeyi yighu xidon'et'onh.
"Gogide viq'iditetal go sighu dhedo hingo.
Ngo getiy ngighun' srigidasdhet," yiłne.
"Yixudz xiday go gogide yixudz go idiq'utth yixudz sitth'in ntodił.
Ts'ixiq'i saxa nixudalningh.
Tr'inay yił axa xiday go iłt'e si'ot che yił getiy xełedz.
Yixudz ye dinayił dina longh ts'ixiq'i dina axa xudhi'onh.
Sighu vixedhinix yixudz, dighusnax ts'ixadinh," yiłne.
Ts'an axaxiłdik "Gila'," yiłne.
"Ngo go ngan' q'idz xits'in' di'elnel ts'in' anh," yiłne.
"Go ngan' q'idz ngiyigg te ye ngiyigg xits'in' n'at dalyoq.
Ngiyiggiy yet vixethtrodhinh.
Niłdina ghogholinh anh in'a diyeloq.
Yixudz xineq'at tugh an'at dran niginetth'igh ts'in'.
Yit chenh niyenxitididix tux
ngidigg niq'ołonh getiy ngizrenh ngi'ot yan' nedr niginditoyh.

Then he pushed the door curtain aside.
Who was this?
A poor, dear old man was there;
a nice, little, very white person[3] was there, and he came inside.
"Ne---," he said to him.
"Someone is there," he said to him.
"Grandchild," [the old man] said to him.
"Whenever I look down on this earth
and see you, I'm very sorry for you.
You are crying in the palm of my hand.
I knew your bones would drop very soon; that is why I've come here.
I wouldn't do this for anyone else, but I think very highly of you.
You were so good to each other, and now your wife is gone from you.
That is why I've done this.
You are lamenting right in the palm of my hand," he said to [the husband].

"Well?" the man said to him.
"I hope what you say is true;
I won't forget what you are saying," he said.
Then he just girded himself tightly, and then he went outside.

There were some caribou skins rolled into a bundle.
There was a marten-skin blanket
that had a caribou fawn skin sewn to one side.
He brought it inside for [the old man].
"Here, you'll sleep on these while you stay with me.
I'm really thankful to you," he told him.
"I feel as if my bones will drop soon.
My time is coming.
I'm so lonely; still, with my wife it was nice.
It was just as if many people were here.
Now that she is gone from me, I don't know what to do," he said to him.
Then, "Come on," the old man said to him.
"She is not anywhere on this earth," he told him.
"She was taken to a land deep down in the water.
Down below is an invincible one.
A giant did it.
He willed her not to make ice cream that day.
He thought that
your pretty wife was the only woman up above [his world].

3. Later in the story we learn that this man is Raven.

Yixudz an'a yiłchet," yiłne.
"Anh n'at diyeloq ine' xiłdi xaxa ditr'oghilax ts'ixadinh," yiłne.

"Ndadz ine' xaxa ntr'ititlchil ts'in' xut'a?" yiłne.
"Viyan'," yiłne. "Ngo' dałine' soxo ni'intełchił ts'ixuyan'.
Soxo ni'intełchił ts'ixaxa ghile'a yixudz dengidiyoq."

"Ngo, xaxa vadinh sitth'in noghidał, sixadinh.
Ngo getiy viq'at anh," yiłne.

"Gogide, sitl'ogh xiyet dingit'adi.
Ngiyigg che idedik enithitrax," yiłne.
"Hingo go chenh ngidedik ngin'q'idz che enaditrax," yiłne.
"Yitongo ngidigg ttheting xiye
gits'i'in ttheting xiyet Yuxgitsiy xut'an itlanh.
Yixodiggi che xelanh ine' dinadheł yixits'in xit'anh itlanh," yiłne.
"Ey!" yiłne.
"Gila'," yiłne.
"Gil xełedz niviłnełtingh, thangidineyh xiyozr gila',
ngo got xilongh ts'in' xighu q'usridineyh
ine' getiy tthing' adinh dingalningh," yiłne.
Ts'an yitots'in yixudz xiłtiy xiyozr gighehon'
xik'idz xiyozr xiday go githoninh.
Yixudz yit nathtanh ts'in' gighehon' xiyozr yixudz viyił tixudalningh.
Deg ndadz sre' viłnałtingh xuyił
xizro lo chenh, "Sitthey," yi vazrne,
"Q'ithe li?"[1] vazrne.
Idiyił nititl'itthit.
"Hingo tr'inisdhit," ne.
"Gila'," yiłne.
"Ngo ngido' go dodo' xindighe'oy tatl-'anh.
Didlang getiy ngitthodh eyighun' drin gitr'itidinoł," yiłne.
"Tr'ideniłquk," yiłne.
Ts'an yitots'in yixudz dichinongil yił yixudz edo' vixitathdlo.
Gan tthingił gan iy tthingił yixudz yixudz xiyinon-giłtr'itr ts'ixiyozr xuyił xiyandiłtux ts'in'.
Tthingił yił xelanh ts'ixe'at.
Noqoy tthingił k'idz axa xiyiłquyh ts'i *all day*.
Che dangan yił xighela' ts'in', noqoy tthingił yan' ło go xighela'.
Yixi yighu' dran vinixiłts'eg xits'in' xidigał xizro lo chenh ghiłghatl

1. Belle comments that these are high words.

So he stole her," he told him.
"He is the one who did it, but [you] can't do anything about it," he told him.

"Is there some way [I] might get her back?" he said.
"No," he told him. "Only with my help will you get her back.
You can get her back with my help, and we'll all be well."

"Well, I hope that my bones won't fall without her [in her absence].
I really want her back," he told him.

"All right, everything is in my palm.
She is down there crying, too," he said.
"And you are constantly crying here on earth," he told him.
"Meanwhile, up there in the sky,
far, far up in the sky, I am a Raven person.
There is another place up above there, above the place I come from," he told him.
"Yes!" he said to him.
"Come on," he told him.
"Come, get a good sleep and eat a little,
because we have a lot of work to do,
and you have no flesh on you," he told him.
So at that, he took a little to eat,
as is good for a person who has fasted.
Then he lay down, and having eaten a little, he went to sleep.
I don't know how long he had slept
when the old man said to him, "Grandchild,
how are you?" he said to him.
He woke up at once.
"I already woke up," he said.
"Come on," he said to him.
"Down below here I saw something standing.
There's a very big spruce tree that we'll work on all day," he said to him.
"We'll cut it down," he told him.
Then they took a wedge down [to the tree].
They pounded it in with an axe,
and they chipped away at the tree.
That was a stone axe.
They kept chipping at it with a little stone axe all day.
There were only stone axes then, because there was no iron.
They chipped all day until dark,

xuyił antr'a yeg noya' iy dindhihonh q'idixiyeloq.
Xiyidenitltsesdi xizro lo chenh,
go dadz yixudz vith q'idz yixudz yeg ndadz xuneg vith q'idz xighundołtsitl.
Axaxiłdik xiyighun' ninedatl xiyighun' tthighatitlquyh.
Xiyighun' tthighititlquyh axaxiłdik,
e---y,
xiyighun' tthighatitlquyh ngidigg che che xiyidinitlquyh.
Gan iy yiggiy yeg niłq'osinalit noti q'idzdi vighun' tithitrit ts'i xiłdi diyeloq.
Axaxiłdik yit xits'i hiłdik xiyiqogg che yiq'anłot'edzgititlquyh venhdida'.
Yi'inxet'ots.
Ts'an yixudz yixudz githon ts'in' go vighu yinedhinh.
"Dingit'a gidhehon ts'i'at?" yiłne.
"Ngo gidhison ts'in' got ngo ngiviva',
xaxa ngivava' isonh ts'ixadinh sitthey," yiłne.
"Ngo go deg go ngin'qogg ghu ngin'qogg ghu xivava' dhison ts'in'.
Ngidigg xivava' yan' ngo iy k'idz dighuginig axa drogg n'isiniyh," yiłne.
"A---," yiłne, "gil ixudz," yiłne.
Giteheł ts'in' yitl'ogiditrik yitongo gila yighun' srigididheyh.
"Venhdida' ngi'ot ngitthe vith q'idz xidingłq'oyh yit
yit yixudz qun' q'i dingiqoyh yit ditoq'un' ts'in'," yiłne.
"Ngidigg, ngidigg xiłdik dixitoleł dixighun'," yiłne.
"E---y."
Ts'an yitots'in' yixudz heyiq'anłot'edzgitlquyh venhdida chenh.
Axaxiłdik yixudz xiyitthe' ititltsenh.
Vitthe' tl'itsenh gan iy łegg nighanithiyoninh.
Ts'an yitots'in' yixudz vitthe' yixudz giliqoy chux tthe' q'idiyeloq.
Yuq yuq vilo yile'idit'iq, xidigał xizro lo chenh yixudz gitthe' itltsenh.
Axaxiłdi ngiyix che che ngiyigg,
vivit yet chenh vidhagg xits'in' ngiyiggiy iy iy xiyet ngiyigg xiq'an'iłquyh ts'in'.
Deg giłiggi no'oy nginh nixunedhit xiq'ixelnig ts'in'.
Gil chenh giłigg no'oy nginh go xiyughun' q'u'idineyh.
Ine' xiłdi yixudz voxo go q'ode diyititl-'an' ts'ixiq'i xinagh vixuxudhi'onh.
"*Hey,* ngo getiy ło'at," inedhinh.
Deg dixet'a ngidigg nigenditoyh tux lonhdi
no'oy łongo ngi'in didhił ts'idz donghidineł dalanh.
Ixuxuyił, "Agidet," yiłne.
"Viq'i'elnek," yiłne.

Ndadz a yixudz łegg chux gilqoy chux q'inyighnitltsenh.
Vichal chux xuyił.
"Gila'," yiłne.

like beavers eating a tree.
They knocked it down that way,
right there on the bank, and it fell nicely.
And then they went to it and limbed it.
They limbed it and then,
e---y,
they limbed it some more and cut the top off, too.
So then he made it about twelve arm spans long.
The next day he started peeling the bark from it.
They went back.
The man realized that the old man had not eaten at all.
"Why aren't you eating?" he asked him.
"Well, I don't eat that food of yours;
I can't eat your food, grandchild," he told him.
"I don't eat the food of this world.
From up there [in my world] is the only food [I can eat]; I brought some of it with me," he told him.
"Ah," he said. "All right," he said.
The man started to eat and gave some of it to the old man, who was very grateful.
"Make a fire down on the bank tomorrow,
and put this food on the fire; it will burn," he told him.
"It will go up into the sky that way," he told him.
"E---y."
The next day they peeled all the bark off the tree.
Then they started to carve a head.
The head was made in the shape of a fish.
Then he carved its head into the shape of a big pike's head.
He shaped it with his hands until finally he had completed the whole head.
Down below
they carved out its insides, its stomach, and its mouth.
An entire month passed without their realizing it.
They worked at it for an entire month.
They thought they were just starting on it.
"Hey, this is too much," he thought.
[Raven] looked up now and then;
the sun was going back to the warm side.
So then, "That's it," he told him.
"It's finished," he told him.

What a big fish; he had made it in the shape of a big pike.
Its tail was big too.
"Come on," he told him.

"Sitthey," yiłne,
"nginh go gil xits'in' yixudz vigitr'itlchidh ts'in'
yixudz iy'in tr'itidiggisr ts'ixuyan'," yiłne.
Axaxiłdik xiyigitlchidh ts'in' xiłdi xiyighun' gitr'otitl'i'anh.
I---y, iy'in gitr'othiggizr dan iy'in xiyidiggisr.
Ngitthe hiłdik tiginiq'at yit xongithit hiłdi neyiniłtanh.
"Gila'," yiłne.
"Ithe vaxa ginatlugh ingit'anh?" yiłne.
"Xo," yiłne.
"Ndadz dingt'a iy?" yiłne.
"Dithiva ts'in' dithitl'idz," yiłne.
"Yan' vaxa ginałtlugh ist'anh," yiłne.
"Gil iy voqo diqondhedoyh iy," yiłne.
Ngidugg tso yanghidiyo ts'in yixi nixititliyo.
Xuyił noqoggiy yixudz yeg vaxa ginałtlugh xiq'iy *powder* xiq'iy
nongholyo.
Axaxiłdi tth'ok k'idz yet xiyitux te ngengił ts'in'.
Xiyił niyinthitth'ax.
Xutl'ogh hiłdi ey axa xiyinitltlux, iy axa xizro lo chenh.
Che yenitltluxdi vit'osin yixudz yiggi dithivadz axa edixi nitltlux,
hingo xiłdi liq'ul axa viginghetl'it q'idiyeloq ło go.
E---y, łegg xit'a chenh ngizrenh.
"Gila'," yiłne.
"Diqondhedoyh chenh," yiłne.
"Gan ditthig ini'a yix idelo.
Getiy doyon chux yił n'at ts'in go ngin'qogg yuxdeyan' yuxt'on-ginisitoyh.
Ngi'ot yił getiy giłdingh," yiłne.
Tso q'i donithiyo.
Gan xizro lo chenh yixudz gimaq yit tr'imazriq hiq'iy.
Antr'a yeg gimaq hiq'iy nongholyo.
"Gogide idisre', idisre' ngighu sregh tiłt'al iy," yiłne.
"Agide," yiłne.
"Agidet iy," yiłne.
Iy hiłdi yixudz ndadz sre' gileg axa diyighił'an ts'in'
yixudz yixudz yinayighelo.
Iy vinayed yixudz n'edidił yit.
Vinayed yixudz yeg nighanoy xiq'i yixudz.
Vinayed niłigits'i q'u'ididał.
Yitongo yixudz yit hinighaldhit got q'idighidhilinh.
"I---y, ndadz dit'anh anh ndadz sre' dit'anh ts'an'a.
"Gil diqondhedoyh," yiłne.
"Diqondhedoyh ts'in tedzeł tthandingditeyh," yiłne.

"Grandchild," he said to him,
"we will tie a rope to it and
drag it over there," he said to him.
Then they tied a rope to it and tried to drag it.
I--y, they could barely drag it, but they dragged it there.
They left it down at the water hole.
"Come on," he told him.
"Do you have anything to paint it with?" he said to him.
"Yes," he said.
"What color?" he asked.
"Grayish and dark black," he told him.
"That's all I have to paint it with," he told him.
"Okay, go on up to get it," he said.
He went up into the cache to search for it.
He found a certain rock, used as paint [when crushed into] a powder,
and he brought it down.
Then they put it in a little dish and mixed it with some water.
He started stirring it.
After that they started to paint.
They painted the back side all gray,
and they painted white spots [like those of a pike] on it.
E---y, it was such a beautiful fish.
"All right," he said to him.
"Go up [to the cache] again," he told him.
"You people have everything here.
You are the richest people in all of the world that I see.
Your wife is so skillful," he told him.
He went back up into the cache.
In it were eyes like large beads.
He brought down those things [beads] that were like eyes.
"Is this all right, I wonder; I hope it's what you want," he said.
"That's it," he said,
"That's just it," he said.
Then he used a medicine song on those things in some way and
then immediately put them into place.
The eyes started moving.
The eyes wiggled around.
The eyes moved this way and that.
The young hunter was very surprised.
"I---y, what is he doing?"
"All right, go back up [to where you are staying]," he told him.
"Go back up and fetch an ice chisel," he told him.

Axaxiłdik yixudz vixighilingithdi nixine'ots.
Niłq'osinal xiyighu tathtrit nodi che viq'idz ło got.
"Gila'," yiłne.
"Go vixaghałchuxdi yixudz tr'atidigguł," yiłne.
Yighu xiyiq'idh yixudz xiyiq'i yik'o ditr'idineggotth, tr'idineggat.
Axaxiłdik "Agidi viq'i'elnek," yiłne.
"Gil diqondhedoyh chenh," yiłne.
"Go dadz dighałchogh etho łats tthandingt'oyh," yiłne.
"Iy hiłdik viyet xa ngingeł," yiłne.
"Iy hiłdi iy viye gineggasr ts'in' iy hiłdik ditoq'un' viyet," yiłne.
"Iy vinedz ditet'el," yiłne.
Iy hiłdik oqo diqon'ithiyo.

Etho łats yozr qunagh xizro lo chenh tthandet'onhdi.
Xa yił xiyighidingił ts'in' ts'ixiłdi yiye dighiłt'onh ngiyigg.
E---y, q'o yitongo yixudz ndadz go ditoneł ts'in'?
Tr'i'enithidhit ts'ixunagh.
Gan ixunałt'a ts'in' dit'anh.
"Ndadz sre' vaxa dixet'anh?" inedhinh.
Ts'an yitots'in' yixudz xiłdik didiyoq.
"Gila'," yiłne.
"Ng'ot nołchidl yiyet q'on-gidiłqon' iy iy yiyet
nevay gan troth gidhith teqaviye dathdloy," yiłne.
Ndadz sre' che che xaxa yanxunighiy.
"Hey," yiłne.
"Ndadz sre' idisre' viye gidathdloy idi hingo dałine' vinixisniyh iy," yiłne.
Yinołchidl q'igighe'ux.
Yiq'igighe'ux ts'i yiyedolneyh
ts'ixuyił xizro lo che nevay ganh trothgi dadz dighontitl'ichux viche' ggudz xelanh.
Yo ngidiggi yo nevay dhith k'idz viye dathdlo dixizro lo chenh.
"Gila'," yiłne.
"Gil vav che oqo diqondhedoyh, viqat gitet'el," yiłne.
"Gon xiłdi iy qay xudhid qay ngi'in qay ngiq'ixitl'ineg hingo hiłdi
ngiyił hatonik," yiłne.
"Yit hiłdi diggu tsisdi'itl-'o hingo vidhagg tr'itehoł," yiłne.
"Yitongo go qunagh ditoq'un'," yiłne.
Go nevay dhith yitl'o dighelo.
Xotl'ogh "Ngidugg che diqondhedoyh," yiłne.
"Nigidinałt'ay tthandigit'oyh," yiłne.
"Iy xiłdik yił ngi'in qay xits'i yi'in tehoł," yiłne.
"Go nevay ganh trothgi ngitl'odaloy yixudz.
Gidey xełedz nganiłnek.

So they walked the length of [the fish] and measured it.
It was twelve arm spans long.
"All right," he said.
"Chop a hole in the ice big enough for it," he told him.
They chopped out a hole the right size beside it.
Then, "That's it, it's finished," he said.
"Go back up [to camp] again," he said.
"Go and fetch a clay lamp about this big," he said.
"Pour some oil into it," he said.
"Then put a wick into it so it can be lit," he said.
"It will be your light," he told him.
Then he went back up for it.

He brought back down a little clay lamp.
He filled it with oil and then got it ready to burn down there.
E---y, what was he going to do?
He was so surprised.
[Raven] had done so much.
"How can he do this?" he thought.
[The man] did as he was told.
"All right," [Raven] said to him.
"In your wife's sewing bags
are two least weasel skins," [Raven] told him.
I wonder how he knew that.
"All right," he said.
"I already know what is in there," [Raven] told him.
He untied her bag.
He untied it and reached inside,
and felt a weasel about so big with a short tail.
The weasel skins in there were from up in the sky.
"Okay," he said.
"Go up and get some food for your lunch," he said.
"They won't discover you away from the village;
[the fish] will stop traveling with you," he said.
"When it lands, you will come out of its mouth," he said.
"This lamp will keep burning," he said.
He gave him the weasel skin.
Afterwards, "Go back up again," [Raven] said.
"Bring back some black birch punk," he said.
"You will go to another village with it," he said.
"Hold these weasel skins in your hands.
Hold them well.

Yałts'in che nigidinałt'ay dangi'oł.
Qay nginixiy yi'in ni'inteholł," yiłne.
"Axaxiłdik gidingidz chux dichighintl'itanh iy
ghonuxsin xiłdi sriłtitehoł,"yiłne.
"Iy nigidinałt'ay xivits'in' xitohał," yiłne.
Gho Yixgitsiy go din'ne.
"Ey'," yiłne.
"Yixudz didene ts'ixuyan' ditasneł," yiłne.
Yiye gheyo ts'in'
yixudz dilo' srił axa gileg axa dighiłan'.
Yit'odz xilditl'idhiyh ts'in' xizro lo che viyił tiyeldhit ngiyiggi.
Ngiyixi te q'atl'o viyił srosr igitr'inelo yeg viyił hididinenh hiq'i antr'an yeg.
Ndadz sre' vaxa dixin'ne antr'a.
Yeg *electricity* din'ne hiq'i viyił ło got.

Viłantl'idag.
Xuyił tr'an'ididhit tux xuyił gihonh.
Gihonhdi xiłdi drogg ni'idiniyh.
Ts'i xizro lo che viyił yixudz dixin'ne.
Ts'an che niviłentl'idaq.
Deg ndadz sre' viyił nigixina'oyh!
Ixuxuyił xizro lo che tr'in'ilighithdi viyił dixiditl'idhikdi.
Diggantl'iggok xuyił xizro lo chenh nugg tsisdinło.
De' eyiggi dinginax ts'in' vazrne ts'in'
nugg tsisdinło yixudz yiye di'iliggok.
Iy tavon xuneg xizro lo chenh.
Yiye dineyo ngi'in qay xits'i
xizro lo chenh ginisrił yołdzighidl yił dit'anh.
Ngo, qay yit q'idighidhilinh vigitiłt'i'anh.
Niyełtaninh inithitraghinh vinighuł.
Giq'idinxitot'eł tr'in'ne yixudz yixezreł ngi'in xits'in'.
Ts'an yitots'in' nginugg xiłdi xitixneyo, yit xiłdi ngine' tadhiyo.
Ane' yiggi
tr'ałtth'e xuchux xizro lo chenh xinxudołtl'ith hingo xiyh yix xut'a che xulongh.
Go yit nineyo.
Yixonix ts'in nineyo yixi gidingidz yixudz dichiliggizr dixitltanh.
Yighonuxsin yixudz xighdiyił.
Ngin'qo xidina' xuyiththag hingo.
Nnn, yit hingo go yiggiy nevay dhith k'idz yidolał iłt'et.
Diyiniłdhinh vazrne ts'in' ditl'ogh, ditl'ogh eyi dathdlo.
Ixuxuyił xizro lo chenh xuyił hingo giq'idinxitidit'eł ginxatolyał ts'ixuyił.
"Vinixiłyigg giq'idinxitidit'eł ts'in'," tr'in'ne.

In one hand you will also hold the birch punk.
You will stop when you get behind the village," he said.
"There is a lot of grass piled in the forks of trees
in which you will hide [behind the village]," he said.
"That birch punk is going to talk to them," he said.
That Raven said this.
"Yes," [the man] said.
"I will do only what you have said," he said.
He went into the fish,
and Raven blew with his hands and made medicine with a song.
He hit the fish on the back and it sank to the bottom [of the river].
Down on the bottom, a humming noise came out of the fish, shaking the man.
He didn't know how the noise was made.
It was like electricity to him.

He fell asleep.
He woke up and ate.
He ate a little bit now and then.
The noise continued.
He fell asleep again.
How long the fish kept doing this!
He woke up suddenly, and it had stopped.
He got up and it had landed on shore.
Just as Raven had told him,
the fish's head was on the shore, and [the man] ran out from it.
It was a nice beach.
He came out from it to a village
where they were hollering and playing ball.
At that village was the man, a powerful giant.
He brought a crying woman out into view.
They were shouting that they were going to have a mask dance.
Then [the man from the fish] went up[stream] in the brush; he went upstream.
Up there
was a big kashim and many winter houses.
He stopped there.
He went upland from there to where grass was piled in forks of trees.
He hid behind [the grass].
Meanwhile, none of the people saw him.
He still held the weasel skins.
He held onto them, as [Raven] had told him.
Then [the people] were starting to have a mask dance and singing.
"In the morning there will be a mask dance," someone said.

Ixuxuyił xizro lo chenh notin niq'ołdałin xiyiggon eting' ts'i xiyołtał
yiggi vi'ot!
Hey hiday niq'ołonh neg!
Yixudz tth'inh ndineghił anh go ło tr'itrigh,
vinighoyigg yixudz nighiditsitl ts'ixuyił.
Go ło tr'itrigh.
Go dotthing tr'ałtth'e xits'i xiyołtał xuyił.
"Ngo donugg ntasoł.
Go donugg gidingidz ghonugg nontr'idiłdi ntasoł."
"Gili ngo yixi ningasriłtał."
"A gil sidavo nididhuxłyo.
Ngo getiy yixudz iłt'e yixudz yisuxteyh ts'i q'usuxłtayh.
Ts'an a enasitrax.
Ngo yixudz disidhuxł'andi xizro dodo istrix ts'in'.
Che q'idong yixughuda' dhitladi.
Ndadz disuxł'anh, ts'i'at iłt'et yixudz?
Iłt'e yixudz siggon' uxting' ts'in' q'usuxłtayh," yiłne.

Nginugg ngiyigg yitongo nigidinałt'ay che ghi'oł.
Iy che ngiyix niyne'onh, ng'in, Yixgitsiy dełne.
Go hingo yixudz yit nighihoł xuyiggi go xizro lo che viqing' nididhit!
Iy yiggiy nevay ganh trothgi xik'idz yitl'odighe'ux.
Ededig che giłigg xididhagg xiyedighe'ux.
Ixuxuyił nevay k'idz ixathdlat ngido' nixutithiquyh.
Ado' yeg nixidiquyh nginixi.

"Q'uthe'?" ixałne.
"Ngo tth'e iy," ne ts'ixuyan'.
"Nida q'untasoł ts'i'at disiduxne?
Ngo tth'e iy," ne iłt'et yixudz din'ne.
"Ngo tth'e iy."
Yitongo ngido', ngido' nixot'usr xiyiggi yixudz
xiyił natathtrit xuyił ngin'qo xudina' anxithilat.

Xiyidhagg noghit'osr yit nugg tsisdinił'o ts'in' xoghogo.
Xiyiye xogighidighił'an'.
Ixuxuyił go iyiggin notin niq'ołdałin nginugg xitathdatl.
De', doyix xizro lo chenh nigidinałt'oy didhi'onh.
Iy lo che go xinayh!
"Dinaghuda' xedhinix!" xin'ne.
"Yixudz yixideq'o'?"
Xuyiggi ngiyiggi tr'ałtth'e xuts'in' xiditl'idingh.

Then two women came, holding a woman by the arms;
it was his wife!
Such a pretty woman!
She was thin from crying;
tears fell from her eyes.
She cried.
They brought her to the kashim.
"I need to relieve myself.
I'll go behind the grass," [she said].
"Okay, we will take you."
"You wait for me here.
You hold me all the time, taking me around.
That's why I cry.
Leave me alone and I won't cry.
I'm already your sister-in-law.
Why do you do this to me all the time?
You always hold my arms and carry me around," she said.

Up there [in the tree], meanwhile, he was holding the punk.
He put it down out there, as Raven had said.
She went there, and all of a sudden her husband was standing there!
He handed a least weasel skin to her.
They each swallowed one.
Then they turned into little weasels and ran downstream.
They ran back into the brush.

"Ready?" [one of] the other women asked.
"I'm not ready," [the birch punk] said.
"How can I go so quickly?
Just a moment," it said.
"Just a moment."
Meanwhile, [the man and his wife] went downstream,
pulled the skins off, and became human again.

They entered the mouth of the fish, whose head was [still] on the shore.
[The other women] were looking for her.
The two women started going inland.
Below was the birch punk.
It was talking!
"Our sister-in-law disappeared!" they shouted.
"She disappeared?"
There was a noise in the kashim.

Ngiyiggi xits'i yitr'itezreł.

"Ngiyetr xitolał a dingit'anhdi, sighu ni'itidhełchilan n'anh.
Sigitiłt'idz.
Yixudz ngitiyix ts'in' xivitasghonh ts'ixuyan'."
Ngitthing yixudz valggats ngitthegh.
Xizro lo chenh yixudz te yan' xelanh xiday go te yan' xelanh,
sanh ło go xelanh.
Yixudz q'o yił yixudz vaxa gitałtizr chux xuyił yixudz tr'iye xighelo yit yixudz.
Ngido' xizro lo chenh gan xizro lo chenh łegg chux nugg tthinł'o.
Xiyits'itathdatl.
Q'o axa dixiyititl-'anh xuyił engtthit ts'i
niłk'ontitl'idhit xizro lo chenh.
I---y.
Axa yił yidithne' ts'in'.
Niłk'ontitl'idhit go yixudz xiyits'ighidił go yixudz
Q'o axa dixiyitoleł xuyił yixudz tidhighit yixudz.
De', ayiggi yixudz viyed yighałtth'aghin
yixudz xiviyił yixudz yiggan non-gidithitux xivigiviyed.
Yixu'egh xontthixitłquyh xuyił yixudz yixi yixudz niłigits'i yixudz q'utitl'itrot.
Dił yan' yił yixudz xiti'ihoyh.
Yi---y, ndadz ditonełin?
Ngi'in qay chenh qay che yixudz diqxune'onh xutl'ogh qay che iy'in ełtrot.
Ngi'o qay xotthegh che q'utitl'itrot, qay xuq'i totth ditathdlo.
Qay xuqul.
Qay xutsedz yan' q'utiyidala.
Xotl'ogh xuyił yixudz tth'anthighith
yixudz xiviyił srosr an gitr'inelo q'idixudiyoq.
Deg xividit'anh xizro lo chenh titl'idhit xuyił.

Xidevo ło got yit ndidhit yitongo.
"Ixudiniy sitthey qay ye, ixudiniy," yixiłne.
"Ngo' axa gits'i dighenaghin ghile che vidisne ts'i'a."
"Qay che yixudz xaxa tthetixune'onh hey iy.
Q'ithe axa vidangine' ts'i'at n'a n'iy."
"Ntoldhił hingo xe che didiyoq ts'i'a.
Gila' ixudiniy," xiłne.
Xidonxiliggok.
"Gil ngidugg, tso yet ixudiniy," yiłne.
"Vaxa xigidalyagh yił yixudz gan a yixudz te łitr te' q'oded yixudz viye ngilitr tthandingdiqoyh," yiłne.
"Ngo getiy dingit'a ło iy," yiłne.

They started to shout for her.

"You won't live; you won't take her back.
I am powerful.
I'll kill them all," [the giant said].
There was a boat by the shore.
Because there was water,
it was summer,
They put arrows and big spears into the boat.
Downstream there, the big fish still had its head on shore.
They went to it.
They started to shoot arrows at it down there.
and it started to back away from the shore.
I---y.
[The wife] didn't say anything to [her husband].
[The fish] started to back away as [the villagers] approached.
As they were about to shoot arrows, it shook.
[The villagers] all got into a canoe,
and it tipped over with them in it.
As they came back up to the surface, the fish started to swim around.
Blood went everywhere.
Yi---y, what will happen?
The fish swam up to where the village was.
It swam around below the village and swamped the village with waves.
The village disappeared.
Only the remains of the village floated around.
Afterwards, the fish straightened itself,
and it began making that humming noise again.
Then the man and woman in the fish noticed that it had stopped.

Raven was standing there [on shore] waiting for them.
"Very quickly my grandchildren, quickly," he said.
"I [had] told the fish not to do anything wrong," [Raven said]
"The fish ruined the whole village.
You should have told it not to do it like that," [the man said]
"It happened when you were in danger.
Come quickly," [Raven] told them.
They ran inside [the house].
"Quickly, go to the cache," he said.
"Urinate on a rag
and bring it down," he said.
"That fish is too dangerous," he said.

Ts'an xizro lo chenh yixudz vinan'
yixudz dił yan' yixudz axa niłinitl'itsitl hingo vighe' yił dił yan'.
Yitots'in' yixudz iy axa yixudz yitthe' tondhi'o yighe' yił tondhidlo.
Yighe' yił xiyetr'anets'ił vighe' q'ul yił xidela.
Ixuxuyił go ghileche go tth'inh gighe' yił yidhaghelo.
Deg ło go dit vinayed yił q'u'ididał.
"Agidet," yiłne.
"Ndagh, ndagh yixi viniq'it tux xi'ogh gighitithnigidi yixi xits'idz gil idinłneyh," yiłne.
"Vaxa gits'i xinin-get'ith ts'ixuyan' xiłdik,
ngichal k'idz zro xitił'eyh iy gitełditth," yiłne.
Gitthi'eldhit.
Ts'an yitots'in' diqonxitithidatl.
Dadz yixudz ton'eldhit ts'i yixudz ndadz sre' vaxa dixet'a.

Diqonxitithidatl.
"Agide," xiłne.
Yiyit yitongo yixudz q'utithinek eyigginh niq'ołonh.
Vanhgiq giq'ux vanhgiq xuyił ghu drintitl'itth'it.
Dinayił q'an-gitldangh yixudz
iyiggi niyidalyoy yił yixudz yadz ntathdlo yixudz.
Q'odet yan' nonxidolyo.
Tth'e yixudz xiyetr'anxideltanh ts'ixuyił yixudz q'ontithinek.
Giq'ux vanhgiq chux ixuyił yixudz yugh ninetth'ax xiłdi.
Eyigginh tl'oditiditr'il, giq'ux tinh yan' ggagg vadr yił.
"Axaxiłdik gogide inigidax yixu ni'enasdił, che go nedhod ts'in' getiy.
Ngixudhil yet dighist'a' hingo hiłdik ngi'ot nghondididhit ts'in'.
Giłixi yan' ngighu ni'enasdił.
Ngo xaxa ngin'qo xudina' xudhil yet nedhodi dighist'i' ts'in'.
Ngo ngidiggi gits'i'in ttheting Xigiyixgitsiy itlanh ts'an got.
Yitots'in' deg xivava' dhison ts'in'.
Sits'i qun' q'udi'alyay yan' xiłdi qaditlt'a ts'an go," ne ło.
"Gogide gitsighath da' getiy xadhinigginh ndigicheth," ne.
"Axaxiłdik ngiyix che niłtreth qageldiq.
Go iy che getiy xathdatl.
Getiy q'idong viye tasitl'e'.
Go iy zro q'atl'ot q'odet sinonduxlo agide getiy yixghu srigatasdheł," xiłne.
"Hingo go viye sinałol go gitsighath ts'id giggoyath ts'id yił viłełting' iy
yił getiy vighu srigidasdhet.
Ine' xiłdik viye sitidhuxłtl'el ts'in'," yiłne.

Its entire face
and its teeth were covered with blood.
[Raven] washed its head and teeth [with the rag].
He cleaned its teeth and made them white.
Then he put teeth-like bones into its mouth.
Its eyes were moving.
"Okay," [Raven] said.
"From now on, stay in a place where there are lakes, where no one will go,"
he said to the fish.
"For people who step there on the ice of the lake,
you will shake your little tail," [Raven] said.[4]
[The fish] went to the bottom.
They went back up the bank.
The fish went to the bottom, but they didn't know where.

They went up the bank.
"Okay," he told them.
The woman started to work.
All day long she made ice cream with fat in it.
She washed her face
and changed the clothes she was wearing.
They got dressed up in new clothes.
They got cleaned up and she started to work.
She made a lot of grease ice cream for him.
She was going to give the frozen fat and cooked game to Raven.
"This is the last time I'll come with you for a long time.
I was here in your world, and your wife has returned.
So I'll stay with you just one more night.
I've been in the world of humans for a long time.
I am Raven from the upper world.
I don't eat this food.
I live only on food that is placed in fire," he said.
"I'm wearing this worn-out marten parka," he said.
"I'm wearing wolverine boots.
They are too old, too.
I've worn them a long time.
If you dress me anew, I'll be very grateful to you," he told them.
"I'll camp in that marten blanket and fawn skin blanket and sleep,
and I am thankful to him [the husband].
But you won't dress me in that," he said.

4. The fish will thus indicate someone's impending death.

"Go venhdi vinixułts'eg xiyoqoyh aghidiyiyh
xiłdik yuxk'odz idantatlnik," xiłne.

"Agide ngighun' tr'etsing' an at didene," xałne.
"Ine' xiłdik siyił tthitux'usr ts'ixuyan'," xiłne.
"Go xiłdik yixudz duxdiyoq xotl'ogh
yixudz ngi'o ngitthegh vithq'idz xiłdik xatuxłq'oł," xiłne.
"Yit xiłdik qun' q'idz xiłdik sital ditux'oł.
Axaxiłdik go dina'ideloy viq'idz dituxlał.
Xotl'ogh xiłdi go vav chenh go vav detthat," xiłne.
"Vav dettha xitthiduxla xotl'ogh go iy vav neg xiłdik viq'i dituxlał.
Yit xiłdi voqo nigidenoq'oł.
Sinxidhuxłnix xotl'ogh," xiłne.
Xiyiyił tthinedatl.
"Ixudzin," xiłne, "Sitthey qay.
Agidet, ngoxo ni'itlchet ts'in'
yitots'in' xełedz xuneg xiłdik nituxdidoł," xiłne.
"Ixudz xizro sinighuł ixudz dinginax dixo'in dingitlok ts'in'," xiłne.
Hingo yixudz viyix niyatitht'an' ngidiggi.
Xizro lo chenh viq'atl'o xizro yixuliq'uł.
Ngidigg ttheting yiggiy q'uth nighuł'iyh viyił tithinek.
Idixunili'on'.

in the morning, as it gets light,
"I'll leave you " he said.

"We love you and what you say," they said.
"Well, just go outside with me," he told them.
"After you do everything,
you will build a fire out there on the bank," he told them.
"You will put my bedding on the fire.
Afterwards you will put the new clothes on it.
Put the food on the fire first," he told them.
"First put the food on the fire, then put on the other nice food.
Then it will all burn.
You'll make me disappear afterwards," he said.
Then they went outdoors.
"Well, now," he said to them, "Goodbye, my grandchildren.
I brought her back for you,
so now you'll live well again," he said to them.
"I did that for you because you would have died in my presence," he said.
Then he floated upward.
It was white beneath him.
He disappeared behind the clouds up in the other world.
That is as far as the story goes.

The Old Man Who Came Down from Above the Second Layer of This World[1]

There was a man and wife. They stay in a side stream and they stay there *year* around. And they are *both* of them really wonderful. And this woman *especially*. She's the most beautiful woman. But she was *really* smart in hand work and everything. And she make *lots* of things. She make bi---g sack of clothes, different clothes. She make all kinds of parky and her husband ne---ver knew about it. Because he always go [out] every day, and when she finish them, she put her man's clothes in one sack, and one sack for woman's. And she has one big cache. She just filled it with all kinds of made clothes. Her husband ne---ver even ask her, "What you do while I'm gone?" He *never* say that to her.

But when he comes back, she got everything ready for him—cooked meat, boiled fish, and sometimes cooked fish. But he can't get along without Indian ice cream made with reindeer fat. It's almost [all] fat, and he just cut it up with a knife and eat it that way with berries. That's his dessert, I think, and he can't get along without it. When he don't eat that, [he] look like he don't eat nothing. That's what he think; he tell his wife. So she make that every [day]. Soon as they finish, she make another one before he comes back. In summertime every day she make ice cream because she don't want it to get spoiled.

Every day she work and cut fish and everything, and in summertime, they both [work] on fish. And when it's time in the fall time, they get lo---ts of berries, but he goes out and gets caribou once in a while for fresh meat, you know, summertime.

But wintertime, mostly, they get lo---ts of meat, and they dry meat, you know, with fat, and that's what they live on. And they have bi---g cache of caribou fat and everything. I don't know for what, they just get so much ahead. Ahead to eat, you know. And that way they just have e---verything. And they kind of are well-to-do. And they have everything [that] they think of or know, 'cause this woman is just too smart, and she do too much work, you know. But her husband don't know it; her husband don't know that she's making so many things.

Well, when he wear out his clothes, she make another one for him and they don't use old clothes, mostly almost new things, because they have too many. They don't want to wear no old clothes.

Wintertime they just stay yea---r around there and just do [what] they do. In the fall

1. After telling the story "Nił'oqay Ni'idaxin" ("The Man and Wife") in Deg Hit'an, Belle retold the story in English. She gave it this new title rather than giving a translation of the Deg Hit'an title.

time, he set BIG line of marten [traps]. Deadfalls they call that. That's when he get marten in. And in evening time he comes back, his sack just full of marten and mink and everything. Sometimes they make threads, 'cause daytime she sews. He never even tell her, "Why you make SO much thread all the time?" Ne---ver.

And in the winter, towards maybe around November, I guess, or October, the ice froze up. And one day she don't feel good. She just wonder, "Why I don't feel good, anyway? Why I don't want to...I feel *lazy*. I just don't want to do nothing," she was thinking. "Maybe he'll get along without [ice cream]," [she] thinks, so she cook little bit for him. [But] she didn't make ice cream. "He can't go without it one night. How many times I'm gonna make it? You know I'm not feeling right," she was thinking to herself. She had some kind of a headache, and she just feel like something's gonna happen to her, but she don't know *what*.

In evening time he comes back. [She] give [her] husband that cooked meat, and they started eating.

"Well," he said, "where's our ice cream?"

"No," she said. "I didn't make ice cream today because I don't feel right. I don't know *how*. I just couldn't *work* today like I used to. So I just keep quiet most the time all day long," she told her husband.

"My!" he said. "I can't *go* without that ice cream. I *want* it. I want that moose fat ice cream and berries. That's [what] *most* I love to eat, my dear wife," he said.

She think to herself, "My, he thinks so much of me. I should have made it for him today."

"My dear husband," she say, "maybe I'll go out and get some snow and I'll make snow ice cream for you right away," she say.

So she took a *dish*, which you always got to bring out for snow, and she got a wooden spoon and she went out. Then she went down on the ice [just to] get snow. She start to go down and she ne---ver came [back] in. My! Her husband start to think, "What became of her? What's wrong with her? Is she in the cache with berries or something?" He went out and started to holler for her, and no*body* [came].

So he went in the house and got a [piece of] birch bark, and [he] light it and he went outdoors. And NO tracks. He went down towards water hole. There was that wooden bowl, halfway thrown in the snow. And he walked to the water hole, and wooden spoon was throwed on the way too. And there's only the water hole.

[Belle whispers] And he was just there wondering, "How could she drown in there or something?" He started thinking everything. And he came in hollering, and [he] hunt in the cache and [found] nobody.

[Belle whispers] He came in [and] he start to cry. "That's my fault. I shouldn't force her to make that [to]night. She didn't feel good and I just force her. That's my own fault," he start to cry. He just cry all night, and towards morning he fell asleep.

Right away [when] he woke up again, he just dressed up and start to hunt all over. Back in the woods where she gets wood, he looks for her tracks. Only her track. Nothing beyond where she used to get wood. And where he come back from trapline, that's the [only] trail. Then he came back. And he started to cry again. Just cry every day. [Belle sighs.] He don't know what to do. He don't even eat. He started to get thin and thin. He feel like eating, but he just start to make himself starve. He wouldn't even go out to that trapline—no more to it. He never even go out. He just make little fire and start to stay in there, and just start to make himself thin. His face got his cheekbone just sticking out, and he feel his hand—nothing but skin and bone.

"My," he was thinking to himself. "It's all right. That's all my fault anyway. I'll just die in this house. I'll starve in here. I'll *never* try to do anything for myself. Much as I *love* that woman, she's gone. That's all my fault," he was thinking to himself.

He was going out and he was getting so thin; he just put something on his belly and tie his belly up, and that way he's standing up straight, and he goes out. He went out to get a little wood, and evening time he sit there crying. After he make fire, it's warm in there, and he just sit there where the fire was before he'll go to bed. His eye was just all swollen because he'd been crying so much. And *all* at once, he hears somebody at the door [who] start to *hit* his feet [to remove] snow. My, he just didn't know what to do. He thought his wife came back. But he didn't hardly breathe, because he didn't know. He never knew there was another people in the world like them, you know. It was only them; they never see nobody all these years they been there. And all at once there was something that was sticking [in the doorway], and it was a *man* coming in. *Skinny* man, just white, skinny man. He look at him. He look at him and that man just look at him.

"My grandchild!" he told him. "You shouldn't cry too much. You know your wife is not dead; she's living in a different world. Then you don't *have* to cry, but you cannot *get* your wife back because there is *no* person will *get* there. The big man got [her] from [here] because he look all [around] in this *second* world, and there's no woman like her. She's the most beautiful and the most *handy* worker. That's why he *took* her from you. And that's his will that she didn't make ice cream. That's how he was going to *get* her. That's why [she] just don't feel like making ice cream that day in evening time. He just came for her and got her. But you cannot get her back because there's *no* way for us to get her back, but I let you know how it happened to her," he said. "I know you was going to die pretty soon, and I feel so— sorry for you; that's why I came. [I've] never come to this earth before, but I decided to come to *help* you," he told him.

"*Thank* you," [the husband] said. "Thank you very much. I'll never forget what you said. Thank you ever so much," he said. And so he told [the man] to stay across [the room]. "I'm going to get something for you."

So he just went to the bench on the other side where their bed was. Bench all around. And he went over there. He went in the cache and he brought one big sack. It was a [caribou] blanket, young one, and marten skin blanket, and caribou skin for mattress, he brought in for him. And he put it down for him.

"You rest on that one."

"Thank you very much. I'll have a good rest. I *never* sleep [in] this good place before," he say. "I'm really thankful that you're gonna give me good, soft place to lay while I'm camping with you."

So [the husband] just did everything, and he start to cook and everything, and he give [the food to the man].

"No," he said, "I never [eat] your *food*. I am very thankful for it but, you know, I am not of this world, so I cannot *eat* what you *eat* in this world," he say. "But still I am really thankful and I'm going to eat it when I go *home*," he say. "In the morning make the fire on the [river]bank and put that food on it and burn it up," he said. "That's [when] it's going to reach me up there, and when I go back, I'll have it," he say.

So, "Okay," [the husband said.]

"Now [I brought] a little food for myself while I live down here with you, and [I'll] eat only my *own* food, what I've brought along with me. This *very* little I'm eating," he say. "Because I couldn't stand this world. I couldn't hardly breathe in it, because up where I live," he said, "no air. Right here too much air, and I couldn't hardly stand it, but I'm going to try to make it *out* with you. I'll try to get that woman *back* for you *some* way."

My, he just put his *hand* this way. [Belle gestures]

"If you do," he said, "I'll *pay* you plenty."

"No," he said, "not pay, no pay. No, I feel *sorry* for you; that's why I come. Don't talk about *pay*," he said. "Because pay, it's no good," he say.

So, the next day, "While I was coming this way," he said, "I found on the bank bi---g tree. We're going to cut that one *down*. You're going to cut it down and I'm going to try to do *something*."

[Belle whispers] And [the husband] was thinking, "I wonder what he's going to *do*, anyway?"

And next morning early in the morning, he just eat, you know, and he tie [a belt around] himself because he's pretty thin. So he got his little axe made out of a *rock* — there's no *iron* [at] that time, just *rock —axe*. And little *chisel* made out of bone and everything. And a wooden hammer, they bring it down. They start to *chip* and beside they *cut* with this little rock axe. It's tied onto crooked stick and they chop it. And a--ll day they were chopping. At last towards evening it fell down because they *chip* it. It's hard to cut with that, and it was *too* big. So they just cut it down and they limb it and it was dark.

"We'll go home now; tomorrow we'll work on it again."

So they went home and they just made fire in there and [the husband was] just *happy*, happy to see that old man, and that old man was *so* good to him. He talk to him, you know, about everything, and he was so enjoyed. And he didn't even think about his wife anymore because he enjoy that old man talking to him, and all at once, early in the morning, they got up again. And they eat again [and] they went down.

He *peel* it, and then they had crooked knife, and they had some kind of a knife. They started peeling; they just drug it along, and they made it twelve feet long. It was twelve times *boghotithitrit* (*boghotithitrit* mean twelve feet). And they *cut* that long. Then he cut the head, too. Maybe with that, thirteen feet. With the head. Then they carve; he start to make a hole in it. And he chisel it out inside. It's made out just like big *pike*. Fish. And he make the *head*. They never knew they work on it a *month*. It's just like *little* while to him because every *day* they go to it and work on it. It's so *big*, you know, and nothing hardly any good to work with. Those days, it's not like our chain saw. And they just work, and they go in the daytime.

"You go for rope, string." (*Tl'eł*, he call that. *Tl'eł* mean a rawhide string.) So they tie rawhide onto [the fish], and they drag it up to the camp. It was getting dark. He said, "We'll leave it here. Tomorrow we'll work on it again. Do you have any paint?"

And [the husband] said, "Yeah. I have some." (Some kind of a color like gray, but kind of a dark green paint. *Łats*. It's just like a rock. Ground-up one.)

"Well, that's good."

"And *liq'ul chenh*," he say, "white one."

They mix it up. My, this old man, he started painting. It turn into beau---tiful fish. And he put little white spot on different places and it made its head.

"You go up there in your house, in your cache where your wife has things. There's a *marble* I think she have. You bring that one down."

He went in there and [said], "I don't know if she have any."

"Well, look for it anyway."

He started to look around there, and [found] *two* marble, just like *eye*, and he brought that one.

"Tha---t's the *one*," he said. And he did something to it, and he put it in [the fish's] eye. My, its eye started to move around, *wiggling* around.

"You see," he said, "it's really a fish now. Well, go and get some kind of a bone. We'll make teeth out of it."

So he make little white teeth out of it. BIG teeth, sharp teeth all over. And he put that in; just *teeth* and everything. He finish that one and after that, he just told him, "You go in the cache again. I know your wife got a *clay* lamp in there. You put oil in there. And put something on it so it'll burn like a candle."

So [the husband] went up and he went in that cache. There were lots that kind, big one, little one, and all just piled up, [those things] she makes out of clay—pots and things. He never knew she make those things 'cause she never tell her husband what she's doing. So he just brought that one, and he lit it and he put it in there.

"Well," [the old man] say, "tomorrow morning you'll *go* in it."

Early in the morning they wake up. "Well," he said, "you look in your wife's sewing bag. There's two little skin in there. I want you to use it."

(What's that? It's a little weasel skin with a short tail. Weasel skin; she had two.)

"That's the one. I'm going to do the magic for you and your wife. When you go up to town, you'll go up in the town walking, and they'll say that they're going to make Indian dance for your wife [to] entertain her, because she cry too much; she want you. Pretty bad, she wouldn't even eat. Every night they had a different kind of an Indian dance for her. And this big man got two sisters. They always hold her, and they bring her in there, in that kashim," he said. "But I'm going to give you this *punk*."[2]

"And [your wife] going to go behind that pile of big grass; the womans go to the toilet. And as soon as they brought her out, she'll say that she want to go in there. But her two sister-in-law will tell her that, 'We'll go with you. We'll hold you and we'll stand by you.' And she'll say that, 'No, I don't want you fellas to go with me everywhere I go. Maybe that's why I cry too much. You fellas are just minding me too much, and that's what makes me cry. You know [I'd] better go back to my place again. Maybe I'll feel better if you wouldn't go with me, and that way I wouldn't cry too much,' she said. 'All right,' they tell her, and all the womans start to go in, and those two sisters, they were standing right on the trail, and she went behind [the grass]. And as soon as she went behind there, her husband was standing there. She just grab her husband, and her husband give her that little weasel skin, and they just throw it in their mouth, and they turn into little weasel, and they just went away, and this punk was [left] standing there.

"Sister-in-law, are you finish[ed]?"

"Not yet; I'm not through yet," the punk say all the time.

They keep saying, "So long you're gone in there."

"No, I'm not through yet. Not yet. Pretty soon."

And they got so tired of it they start to go back [in there]. NObody in there; only PUNK was there. And they kick that punk and the punk say, "Don't do that!" that punk say. That was the one that was talking to them, they were saying. They just start to scream.

"We lost our sister-in-law!" they say. They just run into that kashim and they were screaming. And in the kashim everybody just jumped up. And that big man just jumped.

"You should hold onto her. I told you fellas not to let her go. Why you let her go?" he say. "I'm going to KILL her husband. He's not going to take her BACK from me. That's my own WIFE," he say.

They all went into the big canoes and [took] bow and arrow and something with a stick that they going to [use to] poke it and everything. And they see this fish was about half a mile below. IT was just on the shore. As soon as they went in the water, [the fish] went out and was just floating on top the surface in the water. And he was just waiting.

They were just hollering, "You're not going to live! We're going to take that woman back, and you're going to be dead," [the big man] told that man inside [the fish], but he don't say nothing. But he hear the voice saying that. And all at once this fish just start to go way out. Close they was, just going to hit it with bow and arrow, and all at once, that fish tail, he just TURNED around and he just TIPPED them over. And [the fish] got SO MAD that he just swimmed around. You see only BIG BLOOD; just big swell, cur-

2. Here Belle apparently skips the part of the story that tells of traveling inside the fish. She goes directly to the part about the rescue.

rent. He just *kill* them off. He just went up to the village and start to go around fast. And all the houses, igloo, and cache and everything—nothing but water just [covering] them. Just kill them all. Then he went in the water and started to go home. Nothing left. And [the husband and wife] just stay [inside the fish], and they hear this big noise, just like an engine running, and pretty soon it stop.

Old man said, "Hurry up! Get out of there! I told you, I told you not to kill people. You shouldn't kill people when I told you not to kill people," he told that fish. "You done wrong. Your face and your head, your teeth, it's full of blood. You shouldn't do that. That's against my will you done it."

And he told that man, "Hurry up, jump out! You, you and your wife, go in the cache and get the beautiful dish and towel, skin towel, and hand it down. Good water and I'm going to wash it."

[The husband] just *ran* up there. He wouldn't even say nothing; he just ran up there and did what that old man tell him to do. And he brought it down to him and he just start to wash its teeth. Its teeth clean and white, and its head no bloodstain on it. She just washed.

"I TOLD you," he say, "not to kill like that. You done wrong," he say. "But it's not your fault. They're the one that tried to kill you; that's why you done it. But do not try to kill anymore. Go to somewhere in the big lakes where nobody will [ever] step around. Because you gonna be on the bottom [of] that lake. And if people that don't know come around there, you'll wiggle your tail and the ice will break, and then they'll run away. And that's all." And [the fish] went down [to the bottom of the lake]. "That's finished," he said.

Then they went in the house. "I'm going to camp only one night, tonight, with you and your wife. I got her back for you."

"How [can we] thank you? We're going to pay you."

"No," he said. "You see my clothes? This marten parky, it's *very* old. And this wolverine boot, it's *very* old. I had it a lo---ng time. I want NEW ones for it, for your wife make BETTER than this clothes what I wear. If you dress me up that way, I'll be really thankful for it. You cannot dress me up with it in this world," he say. "But all that food which you put away for me—ice cream, things—you make big fire on the bank tomorrow morning. You burn the FOOD first. Then you put my bundle, my blanket, and BURN it up. And those boots, parky, mittens, cap, everything, bundle it up and burn it too. And it'll come down to ashes. And then you'll see me get out of sight. And it will be, when I get back into my place up there, it will be there just brand new; I'll put it on," he say. "Thank you ever so much."

"Well," that man say, "I thank you more than you thank me because you got my wife back for me. We'll live happiness after in here for a long time," he say.

And that was the end.

Taxghozr
Polar Bear

"That's the one that came over from that other village. It's a brown bear woman. And this [one], on other side, it's a polar bear woman. So he tore up this brown bear woman, tore up his own wife. It's a really good story."

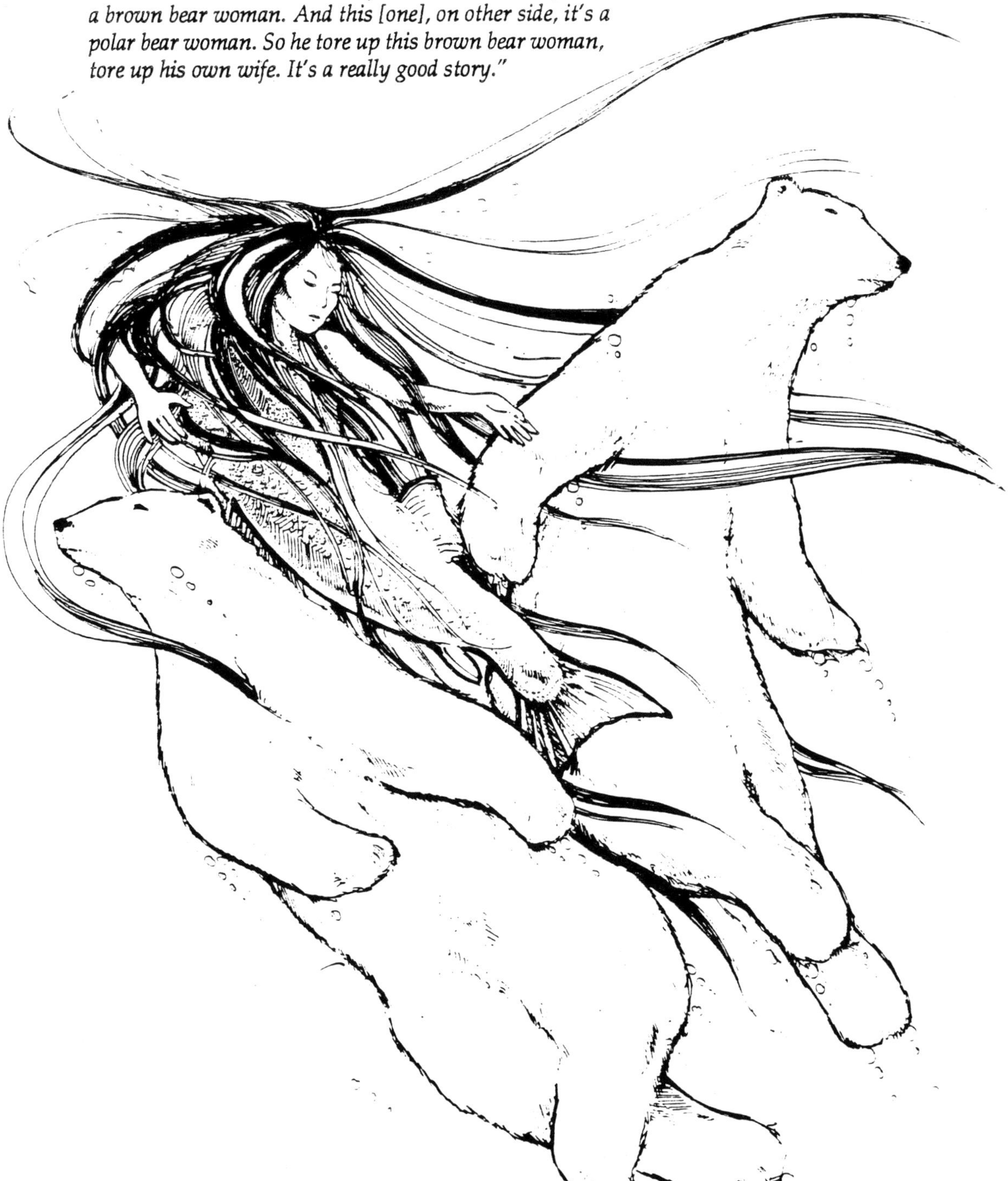

Taxghozr

Qay xudhi'onh tr'in'ne deg tovogh.
Qay xuchux xudhi'onh.
Axaxiłdik niłoqay xiłdik qay xinedr xiditl'itth'e.
Ngido' qun'dochet che che
niłtse sughiluq ye xiditl'itth'e.
Q'idighutux xiłdik qay yi'in'idoyh, anh vitse.
Ng'in qay nixodhił ts'in' xiq'i inelneyh ts'in' iy'odz ni'idoyh ło got.
Yitongo go q'idighidhilinh
niq'ołonh getiy ngichoghinh ghun' dhido.
Viye vigiłt'a' xin getiy ngitl'itth ts'ixuyił ło got.
Yitots'in' ngi'egh genitoyh tux
yit yixudz yiyił ntałtthik yixudz yidhiłgha.
"Ngi'egh niq'ołdałin giye ningł'an.
Gan'a voqo niq'ołdałin q'u'ididałin ningł'anh?" yiłne ło go ts'in'.

Yitots'in' ngi'egh niggon'idiqayh yixudz.
Ngi'egh xuyił gitinithtogits'in' yixudz getiy viq'itr'inighalniy ło got.
Ts'an yitots'in' xidigał ło yixudz,
"Ndadz dingt'a sitiłdhidinh go.
Inagh ing'egh q'u'ididałin nghutl-'an' ts'i go iłt'et siyił tthidixu'oyh,"
yiłne, ło got inedhinh.
Ngiyigg ditrałtth'et xiyen'idoyh.
Tthigitthing niggondili'oyh.
Vedoy chux yet engthi dit'anh engthi.
Ndagh sre' non'idiqayh xiłdi tthigitthing diłanh iy niggondili'oyh.
Gon dixiłdik gon niq'ołonh go vi'ot ngido' qun'dochet
tr'an sughiluq xivits'in' iy giditrik ts'ixuyan'.
Ey hiłdik qat ditthey niłyax.
Axaxiłdik ngideg yixi nixidax.
Ngi'egh xuyił yixudz getiy xiq'a dixet'a dikwil xaxin'nen.
Anh che che getiy vixiyo' ngizrenh.
Axaxiłdik ngi'in genithtog ts'in' xiłdik xighotr'ele ts'in' ło got.
Ts'an yitots'in' yixi yixudz dixet'a.

Polar Bear

There was a village, they say, on the coast.[1]
It was a big village.
And a husband and wife lived in the middle of this village.
At the downriver end of the village,
a poor, dear grandmother and her granddaughter lived.
From time to time, the old woman would go up to the village.
She would go to find out what was happening in the village, and then she would go back home.
As for this young hunter,
a very powerful woman was married to him.
She was tough and very strong.
Whenever he looked around outside
she would suddenly attack him and beat him up.
"You looked outside at other women.
Why are you looking at the women walking around?" she said to him.

Then he paddled up to shore.
He didn't even look about, but he was really getting tired of her.
So at last he thought,
"It would be better if she left me alone.
Why, if I so much as look out at women, she always fights with me,"
he said, thinking.
He went back down into his kashim.
He towed seals to shore.
In his big boat he went hunting on the sea.
I don't know where he paddled, but he hunted seals and towed them back.
Then this woman, his wife, would go down to the end of the village
and give food to that poor, dear old woman all the time.
With that food, she raised her granddaughter.
They lived there a long time.
Everyone liked them and spoke kindly of them.
As for him, he had a good reputation.
He never looked around, because she was jealous.
So, then, things were all right.

1. Belle thinks the story takes place in the Norton Sound area.

Xuyił niłk'ontithiqanh.
Deg dran vadi tr'inxodhił xuyił
xałts'in' xuyił engthit tochox yet
xiyoqo xunił'anhdi angitthet xizro lo che gidithitl'its q'idixet'a.
Niggonghidiqał ts'in' ło got.
Ts'an yitots'in' ngitthegh hiłdik niggon'idiqanh.
Ngi'egh yixudz xiyits'in' tr'idinedatl ts'in' yixi xiyenitl-'an' ts'in' ło got.
Niq'ołdałin yił.
Ngitthegh yixudz tthigithing dhith yixudz getiy long nggon'ił'atl.
Yixi xiyenitl-'an' ts'in' yixudz xiyighun' tr'indidax.
"Gan inałt'ay dił'anh!," xiyinedhinh.
Ixuxuyił iyiggi vi'ot viyenxudolningh!
I-i-y!
Diqing' itidhitlghanh ngitthegh yit.
Che ngidixi xits'in' yixudz dixałne,
"Ndadz deł'aninh anh?
Dingt'a yitiłdhidinh ts'i'at.
Che yighun' dhidoninh deł'anh ts'in' getiy xighoyele," xałne.

Ts'an yitots'in' ngiyiggi trałtth'et xiyentithiyo.
Yeg yixudz yina yił diniłtl'edz ło got.
Yixudz yina yił iłcheth ts'in'.
Axaxiłdik yits'in' xiyen-gidiqonh yehel ts'in' ło got.
Yixudz getiy viyenxughedhit.
Q'ode ixiłdik.
Yixudz deyinedhinh ło got,
"Diyo gidegh tidhisqay ts'in'
go engan ndagh ixindax sitth'in toloł xits'in'.
Dingt'a tidhisqay getiy vigitr'inghoginiy danh.
Ngo getiy viyan' anh yixudz dixighilingith ts'in'
che yixudz xivigho'in qul niq'ołdałin yił ts'itr'ididhisagi ts'in'
hingo che iłt'et sitr'idhiłgha," inedhinh ło go.
Yits'in' xiyegigheqonh ine' gehelts'in' ło got.
"Ts'an gehonh," xałne ine' ngiyix hindinliggit ts'ixuyan' iłt'et.

Yitongo ngido' qun' dochet che
tthidinihoninh sughiluq q'ighididhił di ło got.
Yitots'in' ło got xi'igheyo ts'in' ts'ixuyił ło go yitongo
vitse ghiluq yeniłyaghinh.
Yitots'in' tthanyiłtal ts'in'.
Vinixułts'eg xiduyan' hiłdik tthi'ihoyh.
"Engthit tochox yet gitinighetolan.

Then one time he paddled back out [to sea].
He was gone a whole day, and
in the evening, far out on the ocean,
they looked for him, and far out on the ocean there was a kind of black spot.
It was him, paddling back in.
He paddled back to shore.
All the people came out to the bank and looked at him.
The women too.
He towed a great many sealskins to shore.
They were impressed when they saw them.
"He gets so many!" they thought.
At that, that wife of his got angry again!
I-i-y!
She started fighting with her husband right there on shore.
Meanwhile, all the people up there said,
"Why does she do that, that one?
She ought to just leave him alone.
She's just jealous, doing that again to the one she lives with," they said.

So then he went to his kashim.
In there she gave him a black eye.
She punched him in the face.
And then when she brought food in to him, he didn't eat.
He was very, very angry.
That was that.
He thought to himself,
"I should paddle away
somewhere far across the water to where my bones will lie.
It's better that I should paddle away, for I'm really tired of her.
Well, for a long time now,
even though I don't speak with women,
she has been beating me with no reason," he thought.
She brought food to him, but he didn't eat.
"Well, eat," she said, but he didn't; he just looked down all the time.

Meanwhile, down at the end of the village,
the poor, dear orphan girl was growing up.
She reached puberty, and
her dear grandmother raised her.
She didn't let her go out.
She went out only early in the morning.
"Don't look from shore out to sea.

Ngiyix ngiqa' ningł'anh ts'in' xidongidoyh," yiłne.
"Yixudz an'a ditr'et'a xi'itr'i'usr tux," yiłne.
Ts'an yitots'in yixudz hiłdi dit'anh.
Vinixiłts'eg tr'inedhit go q'udighidhilinh.
Ngitthegh hiłdi vedoy chux dhitonh, ti'ogg chux viye dhitonh.
Ey hiłdi ghun' nineyo.
Ey hiłdi tiyighetonh.
Yiyenxititl'iyak.
Dits'id yiyił yixudz ngidugg tso giggiddh tso ts'in yixudz yiyexidinigheggit.
Idighał xititl'i'an' xiq'i yitots'in' engthit niłk'otidhiqanh.
Yitongo ngi'egh yixudz ło go yixudz xathdrit.
Ayigginh xi'igheyoninh tthineyo.
Engthi gitinathtonh ixuxuyił xidithitl'itsdi xi'eyh gininetonh
ts'an yixudz dina yił ntathtrit.
Axaxiłdik ditse nighuł didenel ts'in'.
Engthit hiłdi tochox hingo engthit
vididinek ngo antr'a ye gidithitinh q'idixet'a ło got.
Ts'an yitots'in' engthit hiłdik dran ghiqał ts'in'
dran xidigał xizro lo chenh dongthi nigatidhi'onh di.
Xidigał xizro lo chenh detsan' ts'in' yixudz vav axa thaghidinek ts'ixuyił
xotl'ogh hiłdik nighalyiyh xotl'ogh che ntithiqanh.
Tthidigigheqanh.
Editthet hingo vidithitinh q'idixet'a.
Venhdi che dran nigidiqanh.
Nodi dran ngełixdi tthidigigheqanh.
Che che ntitl'ighatl.
Nodi tthik nodi dran che tthidigigheqanh.
Xuyił toxdi dran xuyił xizro lo chenh engodz ts'in' xizro lo chenh
xitthegh tr'ighinitldił q'idixet'a.
"I-i-y," inedhinh, "Xiday xighun'enatlniq di!
Dogidinh, nugg xuxudet'a'" inedhinh.
Yitots'in' yixudz ixudiniy ghiqał ts'in' yixudz
q'aghiyił xizro lo chenh yixudz nugg ts'in' xits'in' ghiqał di.
Do'egh yitongo vigho'egh tthigitthing yił tiłevay yił q'u'ili'ał.
Yits'in' genithtog ts'in' yighun' diditlniy ts'in'
yixudz iłt'et iłt'e ghiqał ndadz diyitiłdhel?
Ts'an nuggineqanh yitots'in' tovon xuneg ngine' tidhiqanh.
Deg ngine' ghiqał.
Ixuxuyił xizro lo chenh donugg ts'in' xizro lo chenh xuditidhi'odi.
Yit xudoy hiłdik nineqanh.
Yit ghałton' ło got.
Xotl'ogh xuyił hiłdik diyinedhinh,

Just keep looking down at your feet and come back in," she told her.
"That is how we [behave] whenever we menstruate," she told her.
So she did just that.
Early one morning the young hunter got up.
There on the beach was his big boat, with his big paddle in it.
He went down to it there.
He launched it in the water.
He started to load it.
He stuffed it full with all his blankets and all the furs from his cache.
As it was just starting to get light, he paddled away from shore.
Meanwhile, in the village, everyone lay sleeping.
The one who was menstruating went out.
She looked out on the ocean and saw a black spot on the horizon,
so she quickly averted her eyes.
But then she did not tell her grandmother.
Then out onto the ocean, outward
he moved, on water so calm it seemed frozen.
Then he paddled out to sea all day,
until at last the sun started to set in the west.
At last, being hungry, he ate some food,
and after that he rested, and then he started paddling again.
He paddled all night.
All night it was as calm as if it were frozen.
The next day he paddled all day again.
For two days and one night he paddled.
Once again, it started to get dark.
Poor thing, he paddled this way for two more nights and two days.
Then on the third day, at last, far across the water, he saw
signs of the shore appearing.
"I-i-y," he thought, "How tired I am!
Thanks! Land is visible," he thought.
He kept paddling quickly until
very soon there he was, paddling right up to the shore.
Meanwhile, all around him seals and whales were swimming about.
He didn't look at them or pay any attention to them,
he just kept paddling; what else could he do?
He paddled to shore and landed on a nice beach.
He paddled on upstream [on a river there].
And just then, there, back from the shore, there was a slough.
He paddled to its mouth.
He stood still there.
After a while he thought to himself,

"Dingt'a donugg dichidhisqay donugg giq'i xizrenh di.
Ngidigg sitth'in tołoł di hilay xoqo xenatl-'eł," inedhinh.
Ts'an yixudz nginugg tidhiqanh.
Nginugg tthiłdi ithqay di
xizro lo chenh ganh anugg xizro lo chenh yixudz yix dixudhi'onh di.
Tso xizro lo chenh ngidugg che didhi'onh ło got.
Axaxiłyit yixudz "E-e-ey," inedhinh.
"Divasre' dhido di'at?
Dingt'a go siq'i dingt'anh dina edo'di," inedhinh.
"Go dixitl-'anhdi ayigginh niq'ołonh dhidodi viyan'," inedhinh ło got.
Yitots'in' nuggineqanh xizro lo chenh ngidugg xizro lo chenh
niq'ołonh chux tr'iditl'iqot di.
Yinił'anh.
Iy, gitr'ixuq'iy ndadz sre' yiyił xighengo' ło got.
Xiyił ło go dełne,
"Che lo chenh dina xelanh di, go xits'in' dist'anh di.
Ngo sitth'in tołoł di hilay xoqo ngo dadz disnax.
Ts'idina xelanh di xiq'a di'ist'i' ts'in'," ne.
"Gil dalik ts'in' diqudhehoyh ntelyiyh di,
che ndadz didene ts'i'at?
Ngo enehił," yiłne.
Ts'an yitots'in' diqodhiyo.
Gon xizro lo chenh sanh qun xichux xudhi'onh di.
I-i-y ngi'egh yixudz tthigitthing dhith yił yixudz
doghidelodz gan che viquliy.
Yixudz ye ggath yił yixudz axa imedz dixet'a ło got.
Che tixutighedhit ts'in' iggadz.
Axaxiłdi yixudz gitlvatr yixudz yitl'ogidighetrit
lo engodz ts'in xinagh nineyo.
Engodz ts'in yitots'in' qun' q'idz yits'in dalnek.
Axaxiłdi ło go ey, "Gila' axa drogg indineyh iy ngihon.
Ngo enetał di ngo xighu'enałniq q'idengt'a," yiłne.
Hingo, "Getiy gogide,
toxdi tthidigighisqanh toxdi dran chenh ghisqał hingo
inołdisidithitinh ts'ixoghodi."
"Gila'," yiłne.
"Netayh gila'," yiłne.
Engodz ts'in xididhitanh ngo ts'in nathtanh ło got.

Yitongo engan chenh nonxutididhił engan viq'atl'ot
vi'ot i-i-y getiy ło got viyexughedhit.
Ngi'egh qay xiyił xaxa tthidixutidhi'onh.

"I ought to paddle up [the slough]; it seems good up there.
Up there I'll look for a suitable spot for my bones to lie," he thought.
So he just started paddling up [the slough].
He hadn't paddled very far
when he saw a house standing back from the river.
And a cache was standing up there too.
"E-e-ey," he thought.
"I wonder who lives there?
I hope it's a man's place," he thought.
"I hope it's not a woman's place," he thought.
He paddled to shore, and up on the bank
a big woman came slowly out of the house.
He looked at her.
Iy, she spoke to him in the other [Eskimo] language.
Then he said to her,
"I'm trying to go to where there are men.
I am doing this to find a place for my bones to lie.
I don't want a place where there are no people" he said.
"Don't say that; come up here and rest.
Why ever are you saying that?
Come, spend the night." she said to him.
So he walked up [the bank].
A big fish camp was there.
I-i-y, all around outside a lot of sealskins
were hanging up; nothing was lacking.
King salmon and plenty of everything was there.
It was after spring breakup.
Then she cooked and she fed him,
and he went to the bench across the room.
She handed the dish toward him over the fire.
"Come, have a little something to eat.
Then you can go to bed; you seem tired," she said to him.
"That's true—,
While I paddled for three nights and three days;,
fortunately it was calm for me."
"Come on," she said to him.
"Go to bed, go on," she told him.
She went to bed on one side [of the fire] and he on the other.

Meanwhile, during all this time, across the water—in his absence across there—
his wife, i-i-y, got furious.
She went out in the village, wrecking things.

"Xidagh siqing' ngo siqing' sriłtinołtanh!" ne ts'in'.
Ngido' che che qun' dochet videłtthit chenh tso yił n'ondinłning' ło got.
"Ngo sriłtitr'iłtal ts'in' ndadz dingt'anh ts'i'at?" xałne ine'.
Ngido' chet qun' videłtthit ło
yiggi tr'an, tr'an sughiluq hiłdik xivighun' xidineyo.
"Ngo siqing' ixedhnix.
Ngo siqing' sriłtixiniłtanh," ne ło.
"Ngo yuxtidhatlgha sinighił dituxne ts'ixuyan'.
Ngo, sighun' gidegh tithdolanh in'an," ne ło.

"Ndadz didene ts'i'at, ngo sriłtixiyełtal ts'in' anh.
Ago huch'aliyogginh go digguddhinh.
Go, gogide, dixinałt'adi go xinadhoł.
Tthineyodi engthit tochox yet gitinighetol vidisne
yił ine' engthi gitinathtonh," ne ło go.
E-e-y,
"Engthit gitinathtonh engthit engthit tr'oqał di xinighił'an',"
yiłne ło go.
"Agidet, agidet hiq'a didisne ts'in'.
Qay q'idong tthedixunis'onh ts'in'
tthe q'idong yuxdighisne' ts'i'at," xiłne ło go.
"Ngo venhdida' go q'odet yixi tr'iye tr'iye tasoł.
Yitots'in' viq'i tasqał anh," ne ło.
"Agot anh digguddhinh anh nił tr'iye tatltał ts'in'."

"Viyan'," yiłne ayigginh itse sughiluq.
"Ngo yixudz ditidhenel ts'in'.
Ngo xich'aliyoq ts'in' viyed tr'iye tithol ts'in'."

"Ngo idałine' viye yetatltał anh," yiłne.
Ts'an yitots'in' yixudz tr'iye xighelo
ts'ixuyił yiggi digguddhinh xiłdik idighonthi titl'itanh ts'in'
hiłdik engthi tidhiqanh.
Ndadz xaxa inagh xiyatoneł, che getiy?
"Che yuxtasghonh," xiłne yixudz.
Ngit axa yixudz xiyighun' tr'iye yighiłtanh.
Engan hiłdik xividithitinh q'idixet'a.
Ye engan nuggineqanh.

"Where is my husband? You hid my husband!" she was saying angrily.
She rushed down to the end of the village, and she knocked down the cache there.
"Why, we didn't hide him. What are you doing anyway?" they said, but it was no use.
She rushed down to the end of the village, and
she went to that old woman, that poor, dear old woman.
"Now my husband is missing.
Now they've hidden my husband," she said.
"Now I'll kill you all unless you tell me something.
Now he will never [be able to] stay away from me," she said.

"What are you saying anyway? Why, they didn't hide that one.
Here is a corner girl, in puberty seclusion.[2]
Well, she stayed there several nights.
Having gone out, although I told her not to look out to sea,
even so, she glanced out to sea," [the old woman] said.
E-e-y,
"She looked out and she saw someone paddling out to sea,"
she told her.
"Aha...well, I've wanted to know this.
I've been wrecking the village;
I should have spoken to you first," she told her.
"Tomorrow I'll just get a canoe, and I'll go in the canoe.
Then I'll paddle after him," she said.
"And as for this corner girl, I'll take her along in the canoe too."

"Oh no," said the poor, dear old woman.
"You really mustn't do that.
Why, one who is having her period doesn't go in a canoe."

"Well, I'll just take her in it anyway, that one," she told her [laughing meanly].
Then she loaded the canoe, and
putting that corner girl in the canoe in front of her,
she paddled out to sea.
How could they stop her?
"I'll kill you guys," she told them.
Terrified, they just put [the corner girl] into the canoe.
All the way across [the sea], then, it seemed calm to them.
Far across, she paddled over to shore.

2. The term "corner girl" refers to a menstruating woman. It comes from the practice of sequestering menstruating women in corners of houses.

Che yixudz xiq'i che idedik dixunałt'a di sre' nadhoł.
Ngine' yixudz gits'in yił getiy ixudiniy ło go ghiqał.
Iyiggi tovogh nuggineqanh di done'.
Donigg xizro lo chenh dichixudhi'odi.

Ixuxuyił go che anh che xivighun'
nixutididhił.
"De' agidet," yiłne.
"Ngi'ot, ngi'ot xiyo' didiyoq.
Yitots'in' ngi'ot ngiq'igheqanh.
Ine' hiłdi tthitidhehol ts'in'.
Ts'id ghoyix xinagh xiyetehoł, hingo sideyan' vatasoł."

Yitots'in', "Ndadz i'at donłi tr'itoldheł ts'in'?
Ngo q'idong itlchet, sidenagh an'a ngitlchet.
Sidenagh itlchet iy ngo idałine' getiy viyan' ngo
getiy q'idong xits'in vighun' tasdo.
Yitots'in' getiy vighun' denisdhinh
eni'an'at getiy iłt'et yixudz siyił tthidixu'oyh dixo'in
xidigał xizro lo chenh vidasinix ts'in' go dadz disiyoq," ne.

Deg dixet'a xuyił xizro lo chenh vixighehox di go yigginh niq'ołonh,
ngo xi'ogh nineqanh.
"Xi'ogh noghiqał.
Yixudz an go didisne," yiłne.
Yitots'in' "Tthat tthigheyo'an," yiłne.
Deg dixet'a xizro lo chenh xidon'iliggok di.
"Ngitthe gidet dichidhiqanh ngitthe
gidet vedoy tr'itidhighił," yiłne.
Mmm.
Ts'an yitots'in' "Vedoy chux tr'itithiquyh," yiłne.
"Angiyix tał dhidloy ghoyix xiyengihoyh,
ngo ndadz sre' donłitr'itoldheł ts'in'
ndadz i'at ghodit idetthat siyił titl'itthit an'at viyił tthidixutas'oł," yiłne.

Axaxiłdik ngitthe xizro lo chenh nugg xits'in' goghił hingo,
"Yey...," vazrne engitthedz.
"Adey' siqing' sighun' ingłchet ts'i'at.
Ngiyetr hitolał 'at siqing' sighun' ingłchet?" divazrne.

Yitongo ndugg ndidhit.
Ngitthing hits'in' tthidigixunot'ox tr'alts'in' ło go ghihoł ts'in.
"Yey," ixuyił xizro lo chenh vits'in' diqotitr'itl'itthit di.

I don't know how long she spent in doing this.
She was so angry that she paddled along very fast.
She paddled to the beach and on up [to the shore].
There was a slough.

And as for the others [the husband and his new wife], this is
what was happening with them:
"Well, okay," [the new wife] said.
"Your wife, your wife has gotten smart.
Your wife has paddled after you.
You mustn't go outside now.
You go here under the blanket, while I go to meet her alone."

"What will we do with one another?
I already married her, but I married you too.
I already took her [as my wife], so I better not [hide];
I've already stayed with her a long while.
I still love her very much,
in spite of her always fighting with me,
but finally I got tired of it and I came here," he said.

Here, it seems, that woman [the new wife] made a noise [making medicine].
while she [the other wife] paddled there.
"She's paddling along near here.
That's why I'm saying this," she said.
"Wait! Don't go outside," she told him.
Meanwhile, she ran back in.
"She's paddled into the slough, and
her boat is coming out there," she told him.
Mmm.
"A big boat is starting to appear," she told him.
"Get underneath this mat here,
for I don't know what we'll do to each other,
but if she attacks me first, I'll fight her," she said.

Then, down in the water, a boat was approaching shore, while
someone said "Yey...," from out on the water.
"Adey', you have stolen my husband from me.
Can you keep living when you've stolen my husband from me?" she asked.

Meanwhile, [the new wife] stood up on the bank.
She began to descend toward the shore, walking along very slowly.
"Yey," [the first wife] said, and suddenly she charged up the bank at her.

Vits'in' diqotitr'itl'itthit ts'in' yixudz viyił titr'itl'itthit ło got tthidixutadhit.
Yitongo ayigginh digguddhinh ngiyixi
ngiyixi xinagh xiyegheyo hingo
eyiggi go ngitthing xits'in' ngi'egh xits'in'
xuyił xizro lo chenh xatitl'idingh di.
Xidighiłdingh, xidighiłdingh hingo
giq'idixidetth'iq hingo xidighiłdingh.
Deg ndadz sre' ndixidinłnek xuyił xizro lo chenh
xidon'idiyo di.
Go yigginh niq'ołonh,
"Hidiło," yiłne.
"Ngo, idetthat an'a diseloq.
Avanhtegh łonga' ngitr'eva dixoldhiyh ts'ixuyił.
Ndadz axa se dist'anh ts'iło at idetth'at an'a diseloq ini'an'a
sighun' dindiyoq.
Yitots'in' ngitr'evo dititl'idhey ts'in'," yiłne.
"Gil digg ts'id t'ox tr'inehoyh," yiłne.
"Ngi'in tthinehoyh," yiłne.
Yey, ngi'egh xizro lo chenh xaxa tthidixet'onh di!
Ayiggi vi'ot yixudz ngi'egh yixudz
xizro lo chenh vich'il zro nontl'ich'ił ło got.
Vaxa tthidigixinłch'ił yixudz.
Axaxiłdik xidon'idiyo ts'i tathtrax ło go.
"Si'ot," ne ts'in' yixudz tathtrax.
Ine' yighun' nineyo.
"Dodo ngitrix ts'in'," yiłne.
"Ngo getiy hiq'idinengadz gitr'on'ighił'an' anh.
Tr'al se ngi'ot tatlał.
Ndadz didene ts'i'at niq'ołonh tr'otli' ts'ił'at ixudz datane'," yiłne.
Axaxiłdik xididighenek.
Yixudz go deg vilo' vilogheg yił dił yan' ło got.
Xiłdi yixudz niłtoyitlch'ił ts'in' yixudz.
Ts'an ałixi yixudz ałixi nonxiyininłt'it ts'in' yixudz ngi'o xiyinelo ts'in' yixudz,
ngitthet viyed yeyithdloy yił
yixudz nixineloy q'idz yixi dixiyeloq yixudz xiyidiłq'onh ło got.

Ixuxuyił ło go xiyedixiloyh yił niq'ołonh
xizro lo chenh viye dhido, niq'ołonh yozr.
"Kula..." yiłne.
"Kula..." yiłne.
"Kula go lo chenh yiggit tthidinihoninh sughiluq," yiłne.
Ngo njit axa hingo yixudz ngiyixi nghilighith yitongo.
Ts'an yitots'in' yiyiłtanh ts'in' diqonyitltanh.

Charging up the bank at her, she grabbed her and they started fighting.
Meanwhile, down below, that corner girl
hid down in the canoe, while
out by the shore
the ground started to shake.
The place was shaking and shaking and
there was not another sound except the shaking.
After a long time it quieted down, and
[the new wife] came back inside.
The woman of this place,
"It's all right now," she said to him.
"Well, she did it to me first.
Don't feel sorry or be sad.
Whatever I did, she did to me first;
she wronged me.
Don't be sorrowful," she told him.
"Come on now, get up from under that blanket," she told him.
"Go back outside," she told him.
Yey, outside everything was destroyed!
His wife was out there,
and she was in pieces; she had torn her to pieces.
She had torn her up.
He went back inside and started crying.
Saying, "My wife," he started crying.
But she went back to him.
"Don't cry anymore," she told him.
"For a long time she has mistreated you.
I will be your wife.
I am a woman too," she told him.
Thereupon he stopped crying.
Her hands and her fingers were nothing but blood.
For she had torn her entirely apart.
Having gathered all the pieces together and having piled them up,
they took the things down there in the boat,
and they piled them onto it, taking everything, and then they set it on fire.

And all of a sudden, as they were unloading the canoe,
there was a woman sitting in it, that young girl.
"Have pity..." she said to [the new wife].
"Have pity..." she said.
"Have pity on this poor little orphan," she said to her.
She was crouching down there in terror.
So the woman picked her up and brought her up the bank.

"Q'iye indhididhig ts'in',
ngidugg dhedo ngo ngitr'eniłyax di," yiłne.
Hingo iyiggiy yixudz yixudz xitthidighelo.
Viti'ogg chux yił hiłdik vedoy chux yił yitongo ngi'o dhidlo.

Ts'an yixi xatitl'itth'e'.
Axaxiłdi yiggi ghino diłan ts'in' diggi dititht'an' go eyigginh chel.
Yoxo chenh engthit dit'anh ts'i getiy long.
Nggondititl'i'ok nginixi ghinoy yił.
Ghinoy yił tr'an'alyayh ts'in' ixutiy yił.
Ixuxuyił ghile go giyił tr'ixinedhit ło go vidha qul di xizro lo chenh.
"Ndadz dengt'a?" yiłne.
"Ngo engan hiday siqay hanyendagidhiyh ts'an go dist'a.
Agot niq'ołonh idiyił diyili'anh yił
engan ghiluq yixudo xiday sughiluq yeniłyaghinh.
Ndałon vitse yiq'a xiyodił'anh," anh yiłne.
"Heygo che xełedz tr'atitl'itth'e
ndadz didene ts'i'at," yiłne.

"Dingt'a ixan engan yit xunik xontr'ithidal," yiłne.
Ixuxuyił an'a hiłdik viyed yexixughelo giti'ogg chux yit dhitonh.
"A iy viyed vaxa ninisqanh yan' tr'iye, tr'iye ntr'ithtey
axa ditr'itht'an," yiłne.
"Viya...n'," yiłne.
"Iy siti'ogg yan' axa dist'anh da' dixuyan' gidagh srodix."
"Ngo getiy ngideg ngideg ngichox iy ngiti'ogg," yiłne.
Ts'an tr'iye xididał nik'onxididał.
Engthit xivixedhinix xiviyił tthigatitl'itthit.
I---y, dadz an imedz tiłq'odh
totth iy yixudz ye ngidiggiy deloy ngilanh ts'in' gan chux
ts'ixinagh niłiniliq'iyh.
Viyił viyił diniyhdi totth dotonixi dithiqanh xuyił
xizro lo chenh yiggi ti'ogg vititl'idhiyh di.
De' yigganxidithitux.
Ayeg ane' xizro lo chenh xantthighilquyh di yixi tr'ixuneganh.
Vighon' niq'ołonh ngilanh vighon' che łegg ngilanh.
Vitthegh dongthi q'idingit'a vitthegh yixudz dino'ił te qogg.
Angthegh xantthighiliquyh di,
"Choyalim', choyalim'," ditadhine'.
Hingo go ayiggin niłoqay yixi xinontthixitl'iquyh.
Giłigginh xizro lo chenh yixudz an gi'ot xizro lo che anh taxghozr chu*polar bear* .
Viqing' che *polar bear* ngilanh xantthighiliquyh.
Agide xits'in' dixunili'on'.

"Don't worry about it,
you can stay up there and we'll adopt you," she told her.
Meanwhile, she put all those things into the fire.
The big paddle and the big boat were also out there.

They started living there.
The young man worked and started to do well.
He started hunting for her a lot.
He started hauling caribou back from the uplands.
He brought back a lot of caribou.
One day he woke up and his voice was gone.
"What's wrong with you?" she said.
"I just remembered my village; that's why I'm this way.
This girl she brought with her
was being raised by a poor person back over there.
Maybe her grandmother wants her," he told her.
"Hey, we're living here quite well;
why are you saying that, anyway?" she said to him.

"We ought to go across there to get the news," he told her.
So they loaded the boat; there was a big paddle in it.
"Let's use the paddle that I paddled over here with;
let's use that one," he said to her.
"Oh, no...," she told him.
"We will be safe only if I use my paddle.
"Your paddle is too big," he told her.
So they got into the canoe and left.
When they got out onto open water, a storm overtook them.
I---y, it got so cold;
the waves were as big as mountains and
the boat pitched and tossed.
With the fourth wave he paddled through,
the paddle shattered
They capsized.
Up on the waves the child came to the surface, that little girl.
Half of her was woman and half of her was fish.
And her hair streamed ahead of her, floating on the surface of the water.
Out in the ocean she came up to the surface:
"Grandchild! Grandchild!" she said.
At the same time, that man and his wife came to the surface.
One of them, the wife, suddenly had become a big, white bear, a polar bear.
Her husband also surfaced as a polar bear.
All right then, it is finished.

Polar Bear

Once upon a time there was a big village on the coast. There's a big village in there. In the middle there was this man and his wife. They live with them. This woman, she wouldn't even let her husband look at another woman. As soon as he turned little bit towards other woman, she get so jealous and then she start. She just beating him up all the time. And he had to look at his feet. Never look around nowhere because he's scared of her, because she's too powerful.

There was an old lady, and her grandchild was below in the village, and every time that married man goes out to sea, he hunt for seal. Whale and seal, and he kill lots, and he tow them. And then people comes and help him out. On the beach. And they skin it, all those women. They skin it. So they give them lots of whale meat and things like that. And they give this old lady some all the time 'cause she was good, that old lady and that little girl.

But this little girl was start[ing] to grow up. She never came up to the village. [The jealous woman took food] down to them and give them some meat and things to eat. These other womans, they're good to her, but they cannot look at her husband because she's too jealous of him. So they have big kashim where they give a party. She cook lots of meat and she pass it all around to the older people and everything. And that way she has lots of friends, but her husband got no friends because she's too jealous of him. So at last he started thinking to himself, "Maybe I might go away."

One day he went out again, out to sea, and he killed lots and he came back, and all the womans came to the bank and look[ed] at him. "My!" they say. "What a good hunter. He sure brings in lots of things every day." And she heard that. She got really mad and she just beat up her husband, right in front of everybody. "You fellas admire my husband. You're not going to have him," she say to them. So he, he went into the kashim. She brought some food to him, but he wouldn't accept it from her. [She] sit by him and he wouldn't eat. He just feel so bad because his face and everything was just swollen up. She was hitting him so bad and just beating him for nothing. He decided, "Maybe I'll go away from her. I'm getting tired of this woman. I'm going to go someplace where my bone[s] will be. Where I'll die, and nobody [would] even know where I'll die. I'm going to find a good place where I'm going to be laying [down], and that way I wouldn't live. I don't want to live anymore," he was thinking to himself.

And this little girl, at the same time down there, she got pretty big. And she became a corner girl, you know. She had period. At those times they wouldn't look around [at anybody] till one year [later]. They're in the little place and they let them stay, and there's nobody [would] see them, their faces or anything. So she wakes up early in the morning before the sunrise, and she goes out and look around. She look at her feet, but this time she look way out to sea. And she see somebody going way out. She see black thing moving out. She keep looking and [it looked] just like a canoe or something. So she went in, but she never even told her grandmother about it.

Then [the jealous wife] woke up. Her husband was gone. Never come back. And she went to them and she just bust their cache down. "You hide my husband, you hide him!" "No, we didn't do nothing. He's just not around here." She just beat up them people and just start to tear up the village, and pretty soon they tell her not to do that to them because it's just no use. "You know we're not powerful like you. We cannot take your husband away from you." And she went down to the old lady. She told the old lady and the little girl, "If you and your grandchild don't tell me anything, I'm going to kill you, both of you," she said to them. "No," [the old lady] said. "My grandchild, you know we never go up to the village. We don't know nothing." "Well, you must know something," she start[ed] to tell them. Then she grab this little girl: "You know anything?" (You know she's a corner girl. She's not supposed to look around.)

[The man paddled and paddled for three days and he came to a slough. He paddled up the slough and he saw a house. A big woman came out of the house and invited him in. Meanwhile, his wife started to paddle after him. She took that young girl, the corner girl, along with her.]

And at the same time that one woman back there said, "Your wife is coming. You got to hide under the blanket, under our blanket. Because she [won't] leave me alone. She's going to fight with me because she is very mad already. I'm not mad, but I'm going to try my best to do what I can to her. Because I don't know, maybe she'll beat me up or I'll beat her up. But don't get sad." But he said, "That's my own wife. I love her. I love her very much. But I can't. I got tired. That's why I came this way, because I wanted to die someplace by myself alone," he said.

"Don't you ever think that way, because you're going to live with me," that woman told him. Soon she came in and said, "There's a boat coming out around the corner. Pretty soon she's going to land. We're going to start. I don't know what she's going to do to me. If she's not going to bother me, I'm not going to bother her."

So [the jealous wife] stop, and gee, she got awfully mad. She said, "You took my husband away from me. I'm going to just beat you up and tear you up," she [told her].

"Well, try it," she said, this woman. "I never fought before, but if you want it that way, we'll just start in any time you feel like it," she said.

So she just came out and they just started fighting. That place where they stayed, it was just shaking everything. The ground was just [going] bang bang and just no [other] noise, nothing. Pretty soon they were fighting quite a while, and all at once it just [became] calm. And [she] came in that place [and she] said, "I'm finish[ed]. I got ready for your wife. She started it. Now I tore her all up. I tore her into pieces." He say to her, he started crying, "You shouldn't do that to my wife. I love that woman."

"Well, we can't help it. [If] we never do that to her, she'd tear us both up," [she] say. "Well, we'll take the scraps up and we'll put it in one place and we'll burn her up with all that stuff she brought in that boat. We'll pile it up and we'll put wood on it and we'll put oil on it and burn it, burn her up." And so they did that. She wash her hand. Her hand was all full of blood and everything. Her clothes, she took off her clothes and she changed into new clothes. She was a beautiful woman too. And they started to bring things up, and all at once they see this girl was sitting in amongst the things [in the boat]. She pack her up in her arms and brought her into the house. She tell her, "Don't feel bad, 'cause we're going to keep you good. You're going to be our little girl." But her husband say, "No," he say. "She's a corner girl and maybe her grandmother wanted her. Maybe we'll bring her back across, where she belongs to." "Well, I don't know," she say. "I don't feel like going, but if you feel that way we'll go over."

I don't know how long they stayed there, and then they started to go across. She got big paddle, was just like big tree, was the paddle. Two big ones. "If I use this one, we'll be alive all the time. But if we take your paddle, the one you came with, we're not safe," she said. "No," he said. "We'll be safe. Leave your paddle in there; it's too big. That's too big to handle, that big paddle." So she said, "It's your will. It's not my will, but we'll do that. I'll take your word for it. And it's not safe," she said.

So they went out, they started to go out. It was calm weather. Way out they paddle all day and that night, and the next day this big wind came up. It was big wind and the waves were so big it's just like hills. Maybe more than twelve feet high, the waves. And the fourth wave they start to go over, the paddle just bust. And that's the time that girl came up, you know. Half girl, half fish. And her hair, it's hang[ing] down on the water, you know, saying this: "*Choyalim', choyalim'*." From way long time ago. It's going to be big flu [and] that's the [only] time they'll hear me on the coast." [When people had been starving and there was going to be a big flu], they hear it. Some people hear it on the coast, this kind of half fish, fish animal saying, "*Choyalim'*." They couldn't see it but they hear it. Something say, "*Choyalim', choyalim',*" way off on the coast.

And these polar bear, man and wife, they became polar bear. That's why they're on the ice all the time on the coast. That's the story, Indian story. That's the end.

Niq'odałin Notin Nixidaxin
The Two Girls Who Lived There

Niq'odałin Notin Nixidaxin

Niłghuda' ye tr'in'ne nixidax qay xiyozr xixutl-'onh.
Ndadz sre' xits'in' tr'inedaggin ło go.
Nnn, yitots'in' xiviyił gitidał.
Ngitthing xiłdik valgats yił ine' idihanhdał ło go.
Sanhtux xiłdik tixveł tixitlcheth tux tr'itl ngith yixudz xiyił tiditthiyh.
Iy xiłdi axa niłk'ogixinił'o ts'in'.
Yixudz axaxiłdi nalay yił dixił'anh.
Nuq nonxuxi'oyh.
Axaxiłdik xiyts'in' tux che che gag yił oqo nixitit'isr.
Yitots'in' yixudz xiyiqat xiyiditodhil adhin gag yił yixudz
ngiduq che tso k'idz didhi'onh, gitsatl'on tso iy xiłdik yan' xiyenyalyayh.
Vav yixudz vav neg yił genoq'uth yił yi'idit'oddh neg yił yit xiyiq'i din'alyayh.

Xidonxit'isr ts'in' xiłdik gixinditth ts'in' giqałchin yił yixidighoyh.
Łeq'ath giqałchin yił ts'in' łeq'ath da' che edin xiyit'an.
Yitongo nelang yił xithonts'in'.
Ndadz xaxa dixiyeloq?
Nelang xitoheł, łegg yan' xihonh.
Q'idughutux che che vanhgiq xisrghed yił vituxiy.
Q'idughutux che che niłanht'asr yił vituxiy nixintth'ix.
Yitots'in go ło got niłghun' xithitanh.
Xivits'id niłghun' ni'idalnek.
Yit hiłdik xathdo ts'in' xixinayh.
Niłnighuł nidixaghdet'osr.
Yixudz xidigał xizro lo chenh idinixutodhil yixudz q'ixididhił di.
Nq'ołdałin neg yozr ye notin.
"Ndagh ithe sre' dina helanh ts'igo?" xin'ne ło go.
"Nin etley',
xunhdeyan' iy ngin'qogg xiyetr'itodoł ts'i'a," didene.
"Ixindagh che ngin'qogg dina' xelanh xantr'itr'uxuneg."
Ndagh sre' xits'in tr'ixine'ots ts'in' ło got?

Ixuxuyił xilegot dixunałt'adi sre' yixi nixixidołdhił.
Xiyts'in' nixodhił danxutithidhit.
Xiłdik gag yił axa nonxighidinon'.
Dongitthegh che che q'iyltritr yi'odz nixidighayh ts'in'.

The Two Girls Who Lived There

Two cousins, they say, lived in a little village.
They had come there from someplace.
There wasn't anybody with them.
They didn't even have a boat down on the beach.
In the summertime, they would set a net with a long willow pole.
With that they had a net set.
They got dog-salmon with it.
They put up big bundles [of fish].
Every fall the two of them went berry picking, too.
When they had enough berries for them to live on all winter,
they put the berries up in a little cache by the house, a grass cache.
They put all the food—nice food, dried flat fish and nicely cut fish—in it.

They would go back indoors and twist thread and make boots for themselves.
All they had were fishskin boots and fishskin parkas.
They never ate meat.
How would they get meat?
They didn't eat meat; they ate only fish.
Once in a great while they made Indian ice cream with rose hips in it.
Sometimes with blackberries also mixed in.
Afterwards they lay down together.
They rolled up together in their bedding.
And then they stayed there, talking.
They would tell one another stories.
The years passed and they grew up.
Both of them were pretty women.
"I wonder if there are any other people around?" they said.
"There could be;
we can't be the only people in the world," one said.
"Maybe, but we don't know anything about people."
Where did they come from?

I don't know how many years passed as they stayed there.
Fall came again.
Then they put up berries again.
They carried dry willow home from the beach, too.

Engtthegh hiłdi engtthegh xuyił q'ugili'ał ine' hiłdik.
Ndadz go xaxa dixiyitoleł?
Xidigał yixudz dithitinh.
Engtthegh che dithitinh.
Axaxiłdi ng'egh q'uxet'osr ts'in' ng'egh q'uxughidinoyh xotl'o tux xidonxit'usr ts'in' digixił'anh.
Giqałchin yił yixidighoyh gixinditth ts'ixuyił tuxveł yił xidetl'eyh.
Deg dixet'a xałts'in' xuyił xizro lo chenh.
Ng'in xits'in' xizro lo chenh tr'o'usr q'idixin'ne.
Ixuxuyił ło go yixudz niłixitl'iyił yixudz
"*What is it, what is it?* Gan iy? Tr'o'isr xizro lo chenh," xin'ne.
"*It couldn't be; there's nobody,*" xin'ne ło go.
Ixuxuyił ng'o xidoy xits'in' ntr'ine'ots ngiyix dinaqa' ntr'atitlghił.
Yitongo yixudz xinighiłjit.
"Diva anh, diva anh, diva anh?" xin'ne.
Ts'ixuyił diva sre' adit'anh.
Dinaqa' ntr'idighiłghitl xuyił ng'o xidoy yadz gitadhiniq.
Iiiy, diva zro lo chenh!
Chel sughiluq zring anh dithitl'its, ggingh yozr anh.
Anh xiyits'in' genathtonh tr'ixixehal ts'in' dadz nghidiyo.
Engodz yitots'in' engosts'in dadhiyo.
"Yoonet xits'in' dist'anh," didiyoq ło got.
"He--y, dina ło helanh."
"Ago do xist'anh ago dist'adi, yoona' xist'anh agot," ne ło go.
Xighun' k'osin i-i-y xiyik'o' yitongo.
"Diva ło tthan'idoyh da' getiy viq'a ditr'et'i' ts'in' anh,"
niłixidin'ne' yixudz niłchuxinałtl'isr ts'ixuyił ło.
Xiłdik ts'an yitots'in' enathtanh.
Nxenithidrit.
Xeyitl'o gidighetrit xiyozr ło go.
Yiqantodołiy xał ło xiyinedhinh xiyitl'odighetrit.
Gganh tthantodolinh ghile chenh.
Xughun' tathdo' yitongo yixudz xiyik'o' getiy.
"Yixudz dingt'anh viq'a ditr'et'i' ts'in'
getiy dithizringh anh didhiggingh ts'ixuyił anh," xałne.
"Go kel tr'o'itli' ts'ixe'at denuxdaq?" xivazrne ło go che ixutux.
Mmm.

Ts'an yitots'in' axaxiłdik.
Axaxiłdik xiyitl'ogidighetrit ts'ixiłdik ixudedik gixitadhon'.
Yitongo yit nchitr'ititl'ighił ło got.
Ithe nighun' dolinh anh xiyinedhinh yit dhido.

Meanwhile, out on the water, birds were floating around.
But how would they get them?
Finally it froze up.
The water froze up again.
Going outdoors, they did their outdoor work, and after that,
coming back inside, they worked there.
They made boots, they twisted thread, and they made fishnets.
And that was how they passed the time.
And then, one time there was the sound of someone coming.
They grabbed each other and said,
"What is it, what is it? What's that? It's somebody coming," they said.
"It couldn't be; there's nobody," they said.
Just then somebody stopped in the doorway, knocking the snow off his feet.
They were afraid.
"Who's that, who's that, who's that?" they said.
They wondered who it was.
He knocked the snow off his boots and then he pushed the curtain aside.
Iiiy, now who was there!
A poor, pitiful, black young man; he was skinny and little.
They watched him, not saying a word.
He went over to the other side of the house.
"I came from up the river," he said.
"Ye---s, there is another person," [the girls said].
"Well, I'm not from around here; I'm from upriver," he said.
I-i-y, he sat there across the room from them.
"Why doesn't he just leave? We don't want him at all,"
they said to each other, holding each other tightly all the while.
Then he went to bed.
They went to bed.
They gave him a little food.
They thought he was going to leave, so they gave him something.
But it seemed he wouldn't go back out.
He started staying with them, but they really didn't like him.
"We don't like the way he is;
he's too black and skinny," they said.
"You think that I'm no good?" he said to them over and over.
Mmm.

So, that was that.
After that, they fed him again and they, too, started eating.
Meanwhile, he refused to leave.
They were wishing he would leave, but he stayed there.

Niłchu xinałtl'isr.
Ithe "nongidoł nongidoł," vitr'atoneł ine' xinighiłjit ło go chenh.
Ts'an xinathtanh.
Xinathtanh ts'ixuyił xizro lo chenh
xividotuq xiyetr'ighe'ots di.
Xiyik'o' yi'itezreł.
"Ndadz dingt'anh ts'i'at?" xałne.
"Ngo si'ot tuxlał ts'an'a yix itl-'anh.
Go deg ndadz enedz ndadz nigo ghisoł.
Nq'ołdałin yi oqo xinitl-'anh
xiyił yux q'a'iso ts'an adiyux itl-'anh," xivazrne.
"Ngo ngiq'a ditr'et'i' ts'in' nde," xałne ts'ixuyił
xiyiłcheth ts'ixuyił, dałchen da'.
"Ngo getiy gitr'odułt'a ts'ixuyił gołnonh.
Łegg yan' yi'uxheyh.
Yixoxo ggagg yan' ditatl-'eł
giq'ux yan' tuxnołdi dan'a xivitr'atadhne' ts'ixuyił.
Yitongo xitathtrax ts'i xitrix ts'ixuyił.
"Ngo ngiq'a ditr'et'i' ts'in' ngo yixudz dingt'anh q'a ditr'et'i' ts'in'," go xałne.
Yitots'in' xiyighun' niłts'i'idine yixudz xiyidhiłgha ts'ixuyił.
Idighiłchenh yit dhido!
Tthantithdog ts'ixuyił!

Nnn, vinixułts'eg tr'itr'inedhit yixudz ntr'ithitl'enh.
Xałts'in' xits'ixodhił xuyił xizro lo chenh, xał
xał nduxsin xiyetr'ighe'onh.
Gan xizro lo chenh yixudz nelang yixudz giq'ux tinh yan' yił viye dhidloy
ts'ixuyił xivits'in xiyetr'ighe'onh di.
Ngichugh ghinoy getiy lighanh athdlat yixudz iy go yił xivighun' idiyo.

Xiyił xidontr'et'ots ts'ixuyił xiłdik dixivazrne,
"Gila' guxłvatr ts'ixuyił yitots'in' gidegh uxhonh iy.
Yix oxo in'a ixudz dist'anh.
Ditast'eł che yuxutlzrek di si'ot qay dituxlał di," xivazrne.
Yitongo niłixinałtł'isr.
"Viq'a ditr'et'i' ts'in' ts'i'an," xin'ne ts'ixuyił xitrix.
"Dodo uxtrix?" ts'ixuyił xivazrne.
"Chel tr'o—kel tr'ighatla'
ts'ixe'a sik'o' yi'itr'idhuxtrax?" xivazrne.
Idałine' yixudz ndadz go dixitoneł yixudz xiłdi dit'anh.
Xiyidhiłgha ts'ixuyił tthidangith yixudz
xiyiq'andałchith ts'ixuyił idighiłche dhido.

They were hugging each other tightly.
"Leave, leave," they wanted to tell him, but they were too scared.
So, they went to bed.
As soon as they went to bed, there was
somebody forcing his way between them.
They screamed at him.
"What are you doing?" they said.
"I do this so you will be my wives.
I walked all the way here from far upriver.
I was looking for women.
I found you two, so I'm trying for you," he said.
"Well, we don't want you, so go away," they told him, and
they hit him, but he didn't pay attention.
"You two are eating poorly.
You eat nothing but fish.
I'll hunt nothing but big game for you
and you'll eat nothing but fat from now on," he told them then.
Meanwhile, they started crying and they kept crying.
"Well, we don't like you; we just don't like the way you are," they told him.
They said this to each other and they beat him up.
He still stayed there!
He wouldn't leave!

Early in the morning he got up and got ready to go hunting.
There he was with a pack, just as evening was approaching,
and he lowered his pack to the floor.
There was nothing but meat and frozen fat in it,
and they grabbed the pack.
He had killed some really fat caribou, and that was what he came back with.

So then he came indoors and said to them,
"Go ahead, cook it and then eat it right up.
It's for you that I'm doing this.
I'll do this because you are to be my wives," he told them.
Meanwhile, they kept hugging each other.
"We don't like him at all," they said, and they cried.
"Why are you crying?" he said to them then.
"I'm such—such a nice young man.
How can you cry like that about me?" he asked them.
But they didn't know what to do. He kept on getting meat.
So they just kept beating him; even at night,
they kept hitting him, and in spite of that, he stayed.

"Ngo ngiq'a ditr'et'i' ts'in' nongidoł," xałne ts'ixuyił.
"Viyan', *no!*"
Ndadz go ditoneł.
Ixuxuyił xizro lo chenh.

Deg xiy dixodhił xuyił xizro lo chenh che gits'i'in tithiyo.
Che gits'i'in tithiyo yitongo ntsetltitldux i-i-i-y!
Ndadz xiqul ts'ixuyił eq yił axa xiqul.
"Gila' sighuda'," yiłne.
"Gila', vik'o' niłtitr'ith'ozr anh," yiłne.
Yitots'in yixudz packsack chux ye gixighelo ts'in'
nołchidl chux viye gixighelo vav dixiyidinigheggit.
Xingo giłigginh che ts'id yił tidhighanh.
Yitots'in' tthixide'ots.
Ngido' ts'ixunagh yixudz tithi'ots.
Deg ngido' xo'usr doduq srixtl'ot xelanh.
Yit xiłdi yixudz duq xidhi'ots.
Yitongo gatałtthet ts'ixuyił.
Xiviting yixi xuqul.
Yit ngidugg xidhi'ots ngidugg, ngidugg xixidhi'ots yixudz.
Ndagh axa viting?
Deg, xidigał xizro lo chenh ithchax neg xivighun' xine'ots.
"Gil go tr'inithol ngo," getiy xivighun' enatlniq niłxidin'ne.
Yit xiłdi yixudz ts'ivi il yił yixudz xiyixidinigheketth.
Yit xinadhoł di xixidiłq'onh.
Ts'an yitots'in' yit thaxudinek dixotl'ogh
yixudz ts'id q'idixitlcheth ts'iyigg xinadhoł.
Venhdi yixudz xizro lo chenh yixudz tsetl yił gatałtthet
xixudet'an ts'in' yixudz eq yił axa.
Yitots'in' xałt'onxiłt'onh che nixititht'ots.
Deg dran ndadz isre' nin-gixine'ots!
Xidigał xizro lo chenh yixudz xivighun' xeniłniq.
Ngiyix che xiviqa' che gitr'igatithiggisr ts'ixuyił iy
łeq'ath giqałchin viqa' yixudz gitr'igitathggisr.
Ditl'iqon che xolał xuyił xiyinon-giłqut ts'in' ts'ixuyił.
Xidigał xizro lo chenh yixudz xivighun' xenitlniq di.
Deg dixunałt'adi sre' xinadhoł xuyił yo q'anxatitl'iningh di ey!
Ndagh xingith xizro lo chenh q'idixet'a
sithtux lo che go dixit'anh di.
Ts'an yitots'in' axaxiłdik deg ndadz sre' dixit'anh di?
"Agidet," niłixidin'ne.
"Ne dinatth'in toloł di xoqo ngo ditr'it'anh.

"Well, we don't want you, so go away," they told him.
"No, no!"
What could be done?
So that was how it was.

As winter went by, he kept going hunting.
He kept going hunting; meanwhile, there was a big snowstorm—i-i-i-y!
How white it was then—it was white with fog and snow.
"Come on, cousin," one said [to the other].
"Come on, we'll escape from that guy," she said to her.
Right away, putting their things in a big packsack,
they took a big skin bag and stuffed it with food.
Meanwhile, the other one bundled blankets on her back.
They set off.
They started going downriver.
They walked far downriver to where there was a gulch.
They walked up there.
Meanwhile, there was still a big windstorm.
Their tracks disappeared.
They went on up [the gulch]; they kept on walking up.
Where was that trail?
They went a long way, and finally they came to a nice place under a tree.
"Let's make camp here now," they said to each other, both very tired.
Right there, they made themselves soft bedding with spruce boughs.
They made camp there and built a fire.
After they had eaten a little,
they covered themselves with blankets and spent the night.
The next day there was a blizzard blowing
in a whiteout, with fog too.
Right away they put their packs back on their backs and started off again.
All day they wandered—they didn't know where!
Finally, they became exhausted.
Their boot soles were starting to wear out, and those
fishskin boots, their soles started to wear out.
They had their needles, so they patched them.
At last, they became exhausted.
I don't know how many nights they had camped when the sky cleared—ey!
How far they had gone then—
they were in a different place among the hills.
What should they do now?
"Okay," they said to each other.
"We are now where our bones will lie.

Ndadz ixaxa q'agh xuyił?
Xits'in' tr'ine'ots ts'ixuyił xantr'itr'ixuneg xantr'itlnix di.
Ndagh xuyił q'agh nasrot'isr?" xin'ne.
Deg dran q'ixet'osr xuyił
deloy ndadz nne'oy q'idz dontthidz xitidhi'ots.
Engithits'in deg xito'usr xuyił xizro lo chenh
xighu gits'in' gixenetol xividoyix xizro lo chenh dinating xelanh.
"I-i-i-y!"
Yixudz!
Dighuda' yixudz yitlyił ts'ixuyił.
"Sighuda' yozr, doyix xizro lo chenh dinating.
Diva sre' anh?" xin'ne.
"Xiday vik'o' sriłtitr'ine'ots ts'in' tlagg ting xit'al at," xin'ne.
Ngo nginuq xiłdik tr'igighantl'itits xiq'i
yit xiłdik xits'in' xo'usr.
Dotthing doyigg gixidenathtonh atthe ayix xizro lo chenh xiyh yix xinxighe'o di.
Tso che yin xo'egh dathdlo di.
"Ndadz ixan dasrot'alan?"
Viyan' getiy eyo axa.
"Yit dingit'a dałine' ditr'ititht'ozr," xin'ne.
"Tth'e nigith'oy ts'in' ło go.
Q'idong nigith'ol."
Ngitthing yitots'in' yixudz idiyił vaxitithivanh
Ngitthing yit yitongo yitots'in' yit xiyh yix xidoy nixine'ots.
Ngiyix xiłdi xidiqa' nxatitlghitl.
Xidiqa' xidighiłghił ngiyiq xidixitidhi'ots.
Xidiniłchedh yadz gixinłnek.
I-i-i-y gan xizrol chenh niq'ołonh neg xizro lo chenh dałts'in niq'ołonh neg zro lo chenh dathdo di.
Niq'ołonh tiyh gidi' 'anh.
Niq'ołonh ixan che dighołzrenh.
Yitongo nginigg anugg yux nedr q'ith ts'in' tałghał ni'idalnek ithitth'ix ts'in'.
Gitsatl'on neg che viyiq itlcheth.
Axaxiłdik "Ininga--- sraqay neg," ye xiłne.
"Ndadz yuxaxa dexet'a ts'i'at duxt'anh?" xałne.
"Viyan'," xin'ne.
"Ngo go deg q'utr'et'osr ts'an go.
Tr'athdo di xixotr'itlniq ts'in' yiggiy go deg xitr'et'osr."
"Iningu---, sraqay neg iy, gil engosts'in nux'osr," xiłne.
"Ngo yix oxo gantatlnek di," xiłne.
Axaxiłdik yixudz etho yegighelo nelang yił.
Diyoxo ixan xiyinighuł didithne'.

Which way is home?
We don't know the way back, we forgot.
How can we ever go back now?" they said.
All day they kept walking, and
they came up onto the summit of the nearby mountains.
They went ahead [west];
they looked down below them and there was a trail.
"I-i-i-y!"
There!
She just grabbed her cousin.
"My dear cousin, look; there's somebody's trail down there.
Whose can it be?" they said.
"Maybe it's that no-good guy's trail, the guy we escaped from," they said.
There was a sharp peak sticking up back that way;
that was where they were going.
They looked down below, and there, down at the base of the hill, there was a winter house.
There were caches set up all around it.
"What can we do?"
They were very bashful.
"We should go down there," they said.
"The sun hasn't gone down yet.
It's not going down for a while."
Then they started wading downhill through the snow.
Down there, they went to the door of the winter house right away.
At the doorway they knocked the snow off their boots.
Having cleaned off their feet, they entered.
They pushed the curtain aside.
I-i-i-y, over on the right side there was a nice woman sitting up on the bench.
She was an impressive, middle-aged woman.
She was such a nice-looking woman.
Back to one side of the middle there was a mattress all rolled up.
There was nice woven grass under it.
"Oh my---what beautiful girls," that woman said to them.
"What happened to you, that you're like this?" she said to them.
"No[thing]," they said.
"Why, we're just wandering around here, that's all.
Since we lost the place where we [used to] stay, we're just walking around here."
"Oh dear, you nice children, go over to the bench on the other side," she told them.
"Well, I'll fix things for you," she said.
Then she put food in a pot, with meat.
They should have told her what was wrong.

"Ngo go dadz dina axa dixet'a ts'in' go
ngo' Yixgitsiy dina anh k'o' nigo ditr'it'anh," diyo xiyidithne'.
Xiyidenel ts'in' xuyił xiłdi eyo axa.

Axaxiłdi dze---, xałts'in' nxodhił xiyił xizro lo
chenh ngi'in xits'in dinaqa' tr'itlghitl di.
Ngiduxsin ngiduxsin xizro lo chenh xał dhith chux xiyighets'ok di.
Gan xizro lo chenh yixudz giq'ux yan' dighudinditinh.
Iy yixudz yiye tr'iginelo xizro lo chenh.
Ngi'o xizro lo chenh q'idighidhilinh neg xidon-ghodoł.
Iy chel xit'a chen ngizrenh.
Tilithda' ndathcheth.
Ngiyix che che q'atrek che che
nigighun q'atrek deg xits'in' dighontitl'ingidh chenh ye ithitl'enh.
Ngidigg vanhton che che yixudz nigighun chux nditl'iqon'.
I-i-i-y nda gide yi iłtth'et.
Chel xit'a che ngizrenh!
Yixudz ngiyix xinxidinlggit getiy xidiyonh xidina' yił dadz.
Ts'in xixiditl'inek eyo axa.
"Dina'enił'eyh," xiyinedhinh dadz dixidiyoq.
Yitongo engodz niq'ołonh neg gitiyh gida' "Siyozr," yiłne.
"Go vaxa ndadz dixet'an ngonh?
Ngo giyen disiniyh di dinaghun' nedatlin," xałne.
Tr'ixehal ts'in' nginuq dhitanh ts'ixuyił non'idiyo ts'ixuyił
tritr tth'ok yet hiłdi diyozr ts'i ninineqonh iy xiłdi tadhon' engonh che che
xivitl'o gidighetrit.
Eyo axa gixithon ts'in' ts'ixuyił
yiggi hiyits'in' thodolnek xiyozr ts'ixozro,
nginigg chel anh getiy axa diyonh ts'in'.

Ts'an yit xinadhoł vinhdi che ni'idiyo.
"Na'a," yiłne,
"q'idinengadh ts'in' soxo gitr'ongili'anh, ginighułnik oxo," yiłne.
"Dingit'a diyugh yiggi xividhitlchedinh," anh xiłne.
"Agide dingenisdhinh ts'in' agide xivighun' srigidasdhet," ngoxo yiłne.
De' tthitadhiyo ts'ixuyił
xizro lo chenh ts'id ghał chux xizro lo chenh xidon'et'onh di.
Giggiddh nołchidl chux ndadz dighałchugh chux xidon'ełtonh!
Eyigg engodz nq'ołdałinh ditl'itth'en nił'in dak xivindołcheth.
Yitotl'ogh yit xuyił,
"On," xiłne nginigg dhitonh di xiyighun' ninedatl.
De' notin xelanh ts'in' xiłchet xuyił

"Well, this is what happened to us:
It's Raven that we're running away from," they should have told her.
They didn't tell her because they were so ashamed.

As it was getting to be evening,
there was the sound of someone cleaning his boots up above.
Through the smoke hole above, a big packsack was lowered down to them.
It was full of nothing but frozen fat.
She took some out.
A handsome young man came in from outside.
He was quite handsome.
He was wearing a ground squirrel parka.
He was dressed in long fur boots,
wolf boots up to here [his hips].
His parka ruff, too, was sewn with long-haired wolf.
I-i-i-y, it made him look so handsome.
What a fine-looking young man!
They kept their faces down, becoming shy.
They covered their faces in shyness.
"He might look at us," they thought, so they did that.
Across there, the handsome woman said to him, "My son."
"How did they get here?
Well, I had hoped that someone would come to us," he said.
Without saying anything [else], he went back to where he slept,
and she gave her son food in a wooden dish, and when he started eating,
she gave them some too.
For a long time they hadn't eaten, so
they put only a little bit of it into their mouths,
being so bashful around that young man.

They spent the night there, and in the morning he came back.
"Mother," he said to her,
"for a long time you've done everything for me, cooking for me." he said.
"Maybe I should take them both as wives," he said of them.
"I was just thinking that. I'm very thankful for them," she said to him.
She went outside
and brought back in a big bundle of blankets.
She brought in a big sack of furs—how very big it was!
She gave each of the girls sitting there parkas to put on.
After that,
"Come," he said to them, and they went over to where he slept.
He took both of them as his wives,

xizro lo chenh yitin dixot'an ts'in' yidong.
Notin yan' ghun' xiditl'itth'e, vaxa xełedz xidhi'onh.
Ts'an xidivadr ghun' q'uxitithinek
xivighun' tonik ts'in' ts'an yixudz xiyighun' xiłzrek.
Deg diyo ixan xiyinighuł didithne',
"Ngo go Yuxgitsiy tlaq dinaghun' neyoninh.
"Ngine' xits'in dist'anh,' nen dinaghun' neyonh
anh k'o' an'a
go ditr'it'anh."
Viyił ngidiniyh anh diyo xiyidithne'.
Xiyidithne' ts'in' idivenhditux gits'i'in tidoyh.
Xiydi xodhił xilegg xits'in' xodhił
xuyił xizro lo chenh che digitritr xał xał yit dathdloy ghinontithiyo.
Ixuxuyił xizro lo chenh ngi'odz xizro lo chenh tr'iditisr di.
"Ithe dina, dina engiłtthayh?" vazrne.
"Gogide xiydi gighistrix ts'an go iłt'e istrix ts'in' xiydi ginighidinisr.
Sidadrqay ye sriłtinedatlin.
Sik'o' sriłtinedatlin inixudhitlnix," xivazrne.
"Diyo ixan diyidiłdhik.
An lo che an dinaghun' nedatlin notin nq'ołdałin dinaghun' nedatlin
ngo ngitthing xiditl'itth'e an."
"Ndadz ixan dixivengiloq?" vazrne.
"Sidadrqay in'an," xivazrne.
I-i-y, chel neg.
Ts'an yitots'in "Gil sinotthin nongidoł hingo giyił sighidiq'on tr'oteł."
Viloy tritr ngith go yiloy hiłdik yixudz dangan dhi'on.
Viyił viq'intitr'itht'ots xuyił yixudz vit'odz gitr'ighiłtits yixudz.
Yit yixudz ndołtsitl yixudz.
Yitongo yixudz ngitthing yixudz yit yixudz viyetrq'at q'u'elneyh
yixudz ngitthing yixudz xiditr'idithitits.
"Si'oqay, si'oqay," tr'in'ne ts'in' ngitthing xits'in xiditr'idithitits hingo
nginugg xizro lo che xiditl'itth'e.
"Si'oqay," xivazrne
ts'i yixudz niq'ołonh neg gitiyh dhidon vighun' ntr'ełtthit ts'in' tr'itlt'isr.
Tr'idhitlghanh che an.
Yitongo, "Si'oqay," xivazrne hingo hiyiq'andilighitl.
"Nde!" xałne idighiłche, "Viyan'."
Iligidze—!
Trix yił yixendizreł.
Getiy xiyiq'axititldhit ts'in'.
"Ithe' vitr'idighene'in anh, idigho gighatili'eł hingo ndadz
isre' xo'in ivazrenel ts'in'," xin'ne ts'in' trix yił nonxidizrił.

for that is what they did in the old days.
Those who were well-to-do always had two wives.
So they started working for their mother-in-law;
whatever she was working on, they would take away from her.
They should have told her,
"Well, this no-good Raven came to us.
He said, 'I'm from upriver,'
and when he came to us, we didn't want him.
That is why we came here."
They should have told her [to watch out for him].
But they never told her, and every day [her son] always went out hunting.
Winter passed and it was becoming spring
when he went out on his trapline again.
Suddenly, there was someone coming quickly toward him.
"Did you see anyone?" [the newcomer] asked.
"I've been crying hard all winter and I'm still crying.
My younger sisters have disappeared.
They ran away from me and I lost them," he said of them.
"They must be the ones who came to us.
Two girls who came to us
are staying down there."
"What have you done with them?" he said.
"They're my younger sisters," [the Crow] said of them.
I-i-y, a nice boy.
At that, "Go ahead of me, I have a spear," [said Raven].
On the end of a large staff was a sharp point.
As the man was walking ahead of him, he jabbed it into his back.
He fell down right on the spot.
Trying to catch his breath,
he went in quickly.
"My wives, my wives," he said as he rushed inside toward them and
there they were, sitting in the house.
Saying, "My wives,"
he rushed upon the nice older woman sitting there and stabbed her.
He killed her too.
All the while he was saying "My wives," to them, while they beat on him.
"Get away!" they told him, but he replied, "No."
Danger!
They screamed in grief.
They began to suffer very much because of him.
"We should have told her so that [her son] could have guarded himself;
we should have told him," they said as they screamed and wept.

Yitongo, "Si'oqay," xivazrne ts'in'.
Yixudz yeg ndadz chenh dixivitr'ighilax.
Ts'an at yitots'in' yixudz ngidugg xonxithidatl ts'in'
idixsin noxiyidiggisr eyiggi q'udighidhilin gin neg an vonh yił.
Ngi'ot hiłdik tso giłiggi nixighe'onh iy yet hiłdik xidixeyinelo.
Xidixiyidineggit eyiggi gigguddh ngi'egh dhidloy.
Yit xiłdi yixudz xixidiłq'onh xiyix qun'xiditltthiyh.
Idixunili'on'.

Meanwhile, he was saying to them, "My wives."
He was so happy to see them there.
They went back up from the house and
dragged the nice young hunter inside with his mother.
Then they took down things from the cache out there and brought them in.
They jammed [the house] full, putting all the furs into it.
Then right there they set fire to it, and burned up everything.
That is the end of it.

Two Girls and Crow Man

Once upon a time there was two girls living together alone. They didn't know where they came from, but they just found out themselves [that] they're living together, two cousins. And they don't even have a boat—nothing. They were small but they do everything for them[selves]. They just make fishnet and then they put it out in summertime with stick. That way they get fish, because they didn't even have boat. And they don't even eat meat or nothing because they don't know how to get it. But they get lots of berries in the fall time and rose hips and salmonberries, blackberries, red berries. They pick for the winter, enough for the winter to get by with. And once in a great while they make Indian ice cream for them[selves]. But they eat mostly this. Dry fish they boiled and they eat even the bone. They never waste nothing because they don't know where they'll get some again, they were thinking to them[selves]. And when they come in they do hand work. They make fishnet, and they make boots for themselves, and when they get tired they tell each other, "Let's walk around outdoors and on the beach, and let's bring wood again."

So they keep doing that year round. In summertime they see something's out there. Maybe they see ducks, but they don't know it was something to eat, you know. They just don't know what it's for. They just play around and they had little cache made out of grass, grass cache, and they keep those berries and things like that in there. And they make a nice mat for them[selves] and they both sleep near each other. And they just have a good time. When it's bum weather they stay in the house. And talking and then they laughing with each other. They don't even get sick, nothing. They don't even know how to be sick.

[Then] one time, after they grow up, they live there all the time. "I wonder [if] there's anybody in the world living beside us?" they would say. "Must be," this one girl say. "Must be. This is a big world. We cannot be only ones living in this world. Maybe there's somebody in the world, but we don't know," she said. "We don't want anybody around anyway. We're not used to people. We don't want nobody there," they said. They were just pretty girls and already growing up. And they made ice cream, and they cook fish and everything.

And it was kinda bum weather so they stay in the house. And all at once they just start to hear somebody walking! And they just grab each other, afraid. "What's that, what's that?" they say. "Is it an animal or what?" And all at once somebody just went to the door and just started to hit his boots, cleaning [off the] snow. And all at once little black man, dark complexion man, skinny man came in. They look up to him. [Then] they put down [their faces]. He went look[ing] around. He tell them "Hello. I came from up the river," he say. I been walking lots looking for girls like you—to marry—

and I been walking lots," he say. And they say, "We don't want nobody. You better go right away. We don't want nobody."

"No," he said. "I'm going to stay here. You fellas live poor, and you going to have lots of meat now. 'Cause I'm going to marry both of you. Two of you going to be my wife." "No---," they say, "we don't want that. We don't want no man to live with us 'cause we're used to staying together, only two girls, and we're doing fine," they say. And they cook and they give him a little bit [of food]. "You eat that, then you go." "I'm not going to go. I'm going to stay here 'cause I'm going to marry both of you." he told them.

So he stay there. And they want to go to bed, but they just didn't know what to do. At last they got so sleepy they went to bed. And this man just came in between them. They start to fight him and they just start to hit him. They box him all up. They tell him, "Go! We don't want you, we don't want you! You got no business to do that to us. We don't want you. Just go." "No---," he said, "I been walking a long ways to get here from way up the river looking for girls to marry. That's what I came for. There's no way for you girls to chase me away 'cause I'm going to have you two girls." So they let him go.

Early in the morning he get up and he went [out]. And towards evening he came back with a big packsack full of meat. Fat, caribou meat he brought to them. He tell them not to eat fish no more, eat that meat because you fellas live on fish too long. They don't want to cook it, but he cut it up and he put it in the pot and he cook it and he tell them to eat it. "Now why [don't you want me]?" he tell them. They just turn around away from him and they say, "We don't like you. We don't want to eat with you. Eat by yourself. We don't want you." And when he go, they say, "Oh my! We don't know what to do. How to get rid of him?" They think, "We'll run away from him some way. I don't know which way we'll go, because he'll go, he'll follow our track again. Let's wait till it's stormy and foggy, and then we'll start off," they say.

[The two girls made their escape from the Crow man, and they walked until finally they came to a house.]

...two or three caches, just big caches right near it too. All kinds of fur hang outdoors. Beautiful place. They go down to it. And they went to the door and they hit their feet [to remove] snow, and after [that] they went in. As they went in, on this side nice old lady was sitting there. "Oh my," she said, "what beautiful girls. Where you come from?" she tell them. "We get lost in the woods and that's how we walk around and we came this way. We never knew there was anybody living beside us," they were saying. They don't even tell [her] that they went away on account of Crow man. They never say that.

"Stay on the other side [of the fire], on the other side, and I'm going to cook for you." And back there was a nice big blanket to roll up with, caribou skin with the grass mat under it. Beautiful mat was—they were looking at it, and "I wonder what is that?" they were thinking. And pretty soon towards evening they hear somebody. They see somebody put their packsack through the [smoke]hole on the igloo place, and his mama got it. "I got it," she say. So he came to the door and cleaned his feet and he came in. My! What a beautiful boy came in! Just handsome boy. He had squirrel-skin parka about this long above his knee and just fur. 'Round here was wolverine. Big wolf ruff. And wolverine, I mean wolf, boots. Wolf this way and the feet was caribou skin. My! They just couldn't keep their eyes away from him. They look at him so much. He's so handsome and beautiful. And tall person. My!

"You cook for them, Mom," he told her. "Yeah," she said, "I'm cooking for all of us, but we were waiting for you to come back. That's why we never eat yet," she say. She just gives some to her son in a dish. And then he eat and she give those two girls something to eat, but they were so shamed [shy] of that boy they couldn't hardly eat. Little bit they just put in their mouth while they do this [Belle gestures]. They even keep their hands in front of their face because they don't want that boy to look at them. He will think maybe they're not good enough for that boy. They never even say they ran away from that dark [Crow] man.

And then two days [later] his mother said, "We wouldn't let these two girls go away. Maybe you gonna marry them, because I'm getting tired of cooking for you and do[ing] hand work, sewing for you. Now they'll take my place and they'll sew things for you and everything," she tell him. And her son said, "That will be nice. And if the girls want it only," he say. " 'Cause we cannot force them." "You want to live with us, live with my son and marry?" "We'll be glad to," they say. They wanted him because he looked so good. So he married both of them. They bring two big sack and then they start, indeed they start to live just happy. [When] the old lady tried to work, they just take the work away from her and they just do all the work. Shovel the snow around the house and everything. And they just live all winter there, and they never try to tell this old lady and that boy [about] this man that they ran away from. They never say.

And [the young man] went, he goes every day to his traps and everything. And one day he went and that Crow man was just coming to him, crying. "You see my sisters? I lost my sisters. My sisters, they get lost in the woods. Do you see them?" "Oh," he say. "Those girls that came to our place." "And what you done to them?" "I married them," he say. "Those two, it's my sister. And I'm glad you marry them, anyway," he say to him. And he had a long spear, just like with some kind of a bone, that they poke caribou with. They kill caribou with it. Some kind of a stick. And he told that man, "Go ahead of me! And I'll walk behind. I want to see my sisters pretty bad," he say. And he started walking. Just soon as he started to walk ahead of him, he just poke him right in his lung. Just kill him. He just fell over. "You marry my wife," he say, and he just kill him. And he went down there and he just kill that old lady too. Those two girls, they were just screaming. They grabbed stick and they club him. "You shouldn't do that to them! We don't want you! We wouldn't live with you even [if] you do that for us." "No, I was the first one to marry you, so you gonna go back to our place, and we're gonna live happily at last, after all," he said.

And then they got that man, they drag him down, and they put him back in igloo house. They put lots of stuff [into the house], and they burnt [it] up, and then they went again to their old place. But they were just really against him for that. And that will be, that's the end. They don't want to live with him after that. "If we only told them," they say, "he wouldn't [have] let that man kill him, because he could prepare for him." But the girls, I don't know why they wouldn't [tell about the Crow man]. They were just ashamed, I guess.

Niłeda Sugiluqye Yixo Dixodałdiyh
Two Cousins Shooting Arrows

"So that's a little short story that they used to tell us, you know. When we want story too much they used to tell that to us. I wonder how you'll remember; it's two little cousins."

Niłeda Sugiluqye Yixo Dixodałdiyh

Niłeda sughiluq ye tr'in'ne nixiniłghon' q'uxet'osr.
Teq'avon xuyił q'ugixidałdiyh.
Niłghun' nigixididluq ts'ixuyił ło go.
Ngidiggiy yan' gixidełdiyh ts'i gixidełdiyh ts'in' xiyoqo nixolyax.
Ts'an yixudz dixit'anh edi dran,
tr'itl q'avon xuneg di ło got q'uxet'osr.
Deg yixudz dixit'anh.
Ixuxuyił giłigginh ayiggi vighuda' ngichoghinh,
ngidiggiy yan' gidełdik xuyił viq'o' ixedhinix.
Xiyoqo nixutitl'iyo edi dran, xiyoqo nixolyax ine' xidigał xiyoqo xinithinek.

Axaxiłdik yiq yiggixinathdo.
"Ndadz sre' didiyoq ts'i'at?" xin'ne.
"Ts'an edi deg ntr'ixutl'iyo
ndadz sre' didiyoq ts'i'at?" xałne.
Axaxiłdik ngitthegh che nixutitl'iyo.
Ixuxuyił xizro lo che yiggiy giłigginh,
"Angtthegh ghilo chenh tiyoteł iy," *he say.*
"Hey, iy hey iy ade q'o' ey," yiłne.
"Ho ngo ey iy, agide engtthegh tiyoteł.
Ine' hiłtiy tiyothtel ts'in' gełuxdi xuyan'.
Dingit'a vits'in' tixunhtidhsoy iy," yiłne.
"Sre' ilingith, gil nidigidhelya yixudz
genht'a nixidinełtayh ts'in' yitots'in' vits'in' tingihoyh iy," yiłne.
Axaxiłdi yits'in' titadhiyo.

Tigheyo.
Ngo gatatle ts'in'.
"Vits'in' niłk'otasoł iy yitots'in' yixudz axa ni'etatlchił iy," yiłne.
"Gila xot dangili'ith ts'in' niłk'oghinghoł," yiłne.
Engthi deg nineyo xuyił:

> "Vigenga yaxa
> enga łax do
> enga yaxa,"

ne.

Two Cousins Shooting Arrows

Two little cousins, they say, were walking around and playing.
They were shooting arrows on a beach.
They were laughing at each other all the while.
They shot arrows way up into the air, and then they searched for them.
All day they were doing this,
walking around in a nice place along the edge of the willows.
They did this all the time.
Then one of them, the bigger cousin,
shot an arrow up into the air and his arrow got lost.
They searched and searched for it all day, but they never found it.

So then they sat down.
"I wonder what happened?" they said.
"We've searched everywhere now;
I wonder what happened, anyway?" they said.
Then they started looking on the shore.
And then, suddenly, one of them said,
"There it is, floating along offshore," he said.
"Yes, there it is, the arrow," he said.
"Yes, that's it, floating along right there by the shore.
But it's not floating along fast, it's just in one place.
I'm going to try to wade out to it," he said.
"If you want to, then take off your clothes;
get all undressed and then wade right out to it," he told him.
So then he started wading toward it.

He went into the water.
And he started singing.
"I'll go out to it, and then I'll grab it right away," he told him.
"All right, but step very slowly as you go out from shore," he said.
He walked out there [singing]:

> "Vigenga yaxa
> enga łax do
> enga yaxa,"[1]

he sang.

1. No translation is available for this song.

Ixuxuyił dełne, "Isda," yiłne, "ndagh xoghat te nil'onh?" yiłne.
"Ngitsisdogga' go ghot te nil'onh," yiłne.
"Ey, gila, ngo gho che tr'an-gatas'oł," yiłne.
    "Vigenga yaxa
    enga łax do
    enga yaxa,"
ne.

"Ndagh xits'in' te?" yiłne.
Ngitl'itr'itl hingo ło go.
"Ngiyixi nginesrin xits'in' te," yiłne.
"Ngo dałine' engtthi nedhot *maybe* itidhełchil ts'in' iy," yiłne.
"Ngo idałine' itatlchił ts'ixuyan' iy.
Ngo che tr'an-gatas'oł," yiłne.
    "Vigenga yaxa
    enga łax do
    enga yaxa,"
ne.

"Ndagh hits'in' te?" yiłne.
"Ngidhan xoghot te nil'onh," yiłne.
"Hingo ngiq'o' angtthegh engitthegh nedha xitiyoteł.
Vighun' tididhenol ts'in' xiq'i dingit'a iy," yiłne.
Axaxiłdi che tr'an-gidine'onh:
    "Vingenga yaxa
    enga łax do
    enga yaxa,"
ne.

Ndagh xits'in' te diteneł, biq didiyoq!
Yit xughusr zro xiginitlq'onh, tadhzreł ayiggi
veda sughiluq, chel ngistl'i hanh.
"Isda yozr!" ne ts'in' nontithizreł
ine' ndagh
yitongo engthegh tiyoteł yiggiy q'o',
xidigał xizro lo che niggon'idiyo.
I mean, nithizrił ts'in' yixudz yixo xits'ititltth'it di.

"Ndadz go ditoneł ts'in'?
Diva siyił q'utodoyh?" inedhinh.
"Dingit'a nginugg tthik'odhisoy ts'i'a' yixudz anixi yixudz...
Go dadz dingit'ay tr'itl iy ghontasoł ts'in' iy dichilggizr tthixightast'oł

Then, "Cousin," he said to him, "how deep is the water?" he said.
"The water is up to your knees now," he told him.
"Okay, fine, now I'm going to start the song over again," he said.
"Vigenga yaxa
enga łax do
enga yaxa,"
he sang.

"Where's the water to now?" he said.
He had his eyes closed.
"The water's just below your waist," he told him.
"It's so far out—maybe you won't be able to grab it," he said to him.
"Well, I'll grab it just the same.
Now I'm going to start the song over again," he said.
"Vigenga yaxa
enga łax do
enga yaxa,"
he sang.

"Where's the water to now?" he said.
"It's up to your neck," he told him.
"Your arrow is floating too far out.
It looks as if you won't reach it," he told him.
Then he started singing again:
"Vigenga yaxa
enga łax do
enga yaxa,"
he sang.

The water became so deep, he went under with a plunk!
Only bubbles popped to the surface, and he started screaming,
that [other] little cousin, the little boy [on shore].
Saying, "My dear cousin!" he screamed again and again [as he walked into the water],
but it was in vain,
while out in the water the arrow floated around,
until at last he came back ashore
I mean, he stopped screaming and fell right down there.

"What ever will happen now?
Who will walk around with me?" he thought.
"I should just go up into the woods and just try to...
I'll go that way to the willows and put my head in a forked branch

ts'in' yixudz nixutagighuł xatidhagigha," inedhinh.
Ts'an nginugg tthik'otadhiyo.
Yitongo iłt'et itrix.
Tr'itl vichiliggizr xelan ił iy ghun' nineyo.
Iy ghun' ditthe' iy diloggizr xuyedinghiłtl'ith yixudz nixatitl'ighił.
De'.
Yitots'in' yixudz xididhitl'ighanh.
Idixunili'on'.

and choke myself and kill myself," he thought.
So he started up into the woods.
All the while he was crying.
He went up to a willow that was forked.
He put his head into the fork of the branch and just choked himself.
Oh.
He killed himself instantly.
That's the end of it.

Tr'an Sughiluq Tthux Ni'idhit'
The Old Woman Who Lived Alone

"This story is [about] a little old woman [who] lived alone. She'd always stay by herself on the side stream where she lives, but she makes out all right; there's a lot of current where she lives. [I learned this story from] one old woman that they used to call Martin Stiles's mother. I don't know what's her name. I was a little kid. Those are short little stories. [She was from] Anvik. You know, they used to come to us because long time ago they never used to have welfare. And they have ha—rd time, those old people. And those people that [had no] food, they come around when we]re going to eat, and my mother and my father never let them down. They come and eat with us. Every time when it's time to eat, they come and they share food with them. So they were so thankful that they want to tell a story."

Tr'an Sughiluq Tthux Ni'idhit

Ideyan' ni'idhit tr'in'ne.
Ts'an yixi nixidołdhił ghiluq ts'i yixudz ggał k'ogidiniłʼo ts'ixuyił.
Axaxiłdik xiyts'in' nonxudidhit chenh.
Tixveł axa idandidiniyh ts'ixiłdi nginixi che q'ontithiyo.
Gag yił yixudz xits'i diningiloq, xiyh xoned.
Ixuxuyił xiyts'in' nixodhił.
Yixi yixudz dingit'a ixuxuyił ingtthit etho k'idz
te nadhil yixudz enitlch'ox, eniłch'ux engthi.

Ixuxuyił xizro lo chenh
xughu gits'i gatetth'el ts'in' ngi'in xits'in' xixuditl'itth'onh di.
Yixudz titl'ighith.
"Gan sre' idit'anh?" inedhinh.
Ixuxuyił ngi'o vidoy xizro che yadz gititl'inek di.
Yi—y gan xizro lo chenh.
Ggagg xizro lo chenh ngi'o xiditthighitthik di gidiłdlot ts'in'.
I—y yixudz titl'ighith, dadz go ditoneł ts'in'?
Gidiłghunh hingo yixudz viyix ges yixudz nixuditlux ts'ixuyił.
Getiy nałjit ts'in' deg yixudz idighanot go ginditoyh gan go yaxaditonel.
Ngiyix che tavasr.
"It wouldn't help," inedhinh.
"Yix tavasr *it wouldn't help any."*
Engthit yiggiy te nadhil.
"Gil go sidho ngałtlot," tr'an sughiluq yiłne.
"Gil gide dats'ix, ngo ngidhagg tagitlił di," yiłne.
Yiggi te nałch'ugh yixudz yidhagg dighiłtsitl yixudz ngiyigg.
Yitoyiq xizro lo che yixudz ngitthidiginilghith yixudz ngi'in diyił nitithitrit.
Vidhagg yili'eq yitongo te nałch'uxiy.
Ndadz go xaxa tthitohoł ts'in', xaxa tthighiyo ts'ixadinh.
Venhdida' venhdida' xuyił tthitadhiyo.
Xałts'in' go digiyeloq.
Venhdida' tthitadhiyo xizro lo chenh
di'o eyiggi vitso' k'idz gitsatl'on tso didhi'onh.
Vigho'egh vighoyixi xizro lo chenh gitathch'id.
Tritr ngith iłchet yigidinetthiyh yił datthon' xizro lo chenh.
Axaxiłdik xełedz yighun' neyo ts'in' yinitl'i'an' datthon' ło got.

The Old Woman Who Lived Alone

She lived alone, they say.
The years went by, and the poor dear always netted for fish.
Fall came again.
She stopped using the fishnet and started walking around in the country.
She picked berries for winter.
Winter was approaching.
As she was doing these things, the little pot
of hot water on the fire started to boil; it was boiling on the fire.

Suddenly,
having not heard anything [previously], from outside she heard a noise.
She was startled.
"What can that be?" she thought.
Suddenly, something pushed aside the door curtain.
Yi---y, there it was.
It was an animal; it stuck its head inside, growling.
I---y, she was startled; what could she do?
Its growling made her little house tremble.
Terrified, she looked all around her for something she could grab.
Down there was her ulu.
"It wouldn't help," she thought.
"That ulu, it wouldn't help any."
Over the fire was that hot water.
"Come, jump into my mouth," [the animal] told the dear old woman.
"Okay, open your mouth wide. I'm going to jump down your throat," she told it.
She took that boiling water and threw it down its throat, pot and all.
Instantly it started flinging its head around, and it ran back out the door.
The boiling water went down its throat.
How could she go outside? There was no way to go outside.
The next morning, she went out.
This had happened in the evening.
In the morning she went out, and
out there her little cache, a grass cache, stood.
Near it, underneath it, there was something lying flat.
She took a long stick and poked it, and it was dead.
She went right up to it, looked at it, and it was quite dead.

Yitots'in' yixudz xidon'idiyo ts'in' yixudz ditavazr sughiluq nigheq'onh.
Yitots'in' yixudz yighun' tthititl'ich'ił.
E---y gan xizro lo chenh!
Dithitl'idz xizro lo che got.
Nda gide viq'ux ngichox!
Xiyts'in' donxidelyoggiy.
Axaxiłdi yighun' tthi'itlch'ił ndadz sre' xoghod.
Axaxiłdik yidhith hiłdi ngi'ot tso tso ghonigg hiłdi doyighidiłcheth.
Ngo yixudz niłto'itałt'otth, viq'ux yixudz ndadz dighałtonh!
Giq'ux xuyił yidinighezriyh yił ginelang yixudz
ethok yeghet'otth yixudz gatitlvatr, xiday go ghiluq.
Yiggiy genoq'uth yan' ihonh łegg yan' ihonh.
Yixudz gititlvatr yixi gitlvatr hiłdi yixudz gitadhon'.
Yitongo ngidiggi tso yet xuyił ngiyiggi tsiginiq'at xiyenyalyayh, go nelang.
Yixudz yixi xełedz nixine'onh yitots'in'.
Axaxiłdi yixi xełedz nixine'onh ts'ihiłdi yixi q'iyltridr yił dił'anh.
Xełedz xineg yixi yiqatathdo'.
Ngo q'ode giq'ux ihon giq'ux neg yił tadhon'.
Yitongo che vanhgiq xuyił nidinditth'ix yił aqat xełedz dhido.
Yitongo che diggi'etthiy q'u'eteyh diggi'etthiy yaxa dit'anh iy.
Hnn.
Ts'an yixi dhido ye xidiq'otth.
Ye xidiq'otth xizro lo chenh ngi'in xidoy xits'in' gidetth'onh di.
Ngi'in xizro lo chenh hits'in' q'utr'et'osr di.
Xidoy ntr'ine'ots di dinaqa' ghotitr'itlnek di.
Deg dixet'a xuyił ngi'o xizro lo che che liggingh xidineyo di,
vinan' dinithitl'idzinh.
"Natsoo![1]
Zruh zruh zruh! Natsoo! Zruh zruh zruh" yatadhine'.
"Dina lo che helanh.
Gile engodz tidhehoyh," yiłne.
Engodz yitots'in' tadhiyo.
Yitongo engthi giłvatr.
Axaxiłdi nuggi yine'onh.
Dit'oxts'in' nuggi yine'onh hiłdi go dit'oxts'in diyiniłqonh.
Tth'ok k'idz yet hiłdi yitl'ogidighetrit.
"Natsoo," yiłne, "ndadz xaxa vidhelan gon?" yiłne.
"Xiyts'in' dong sittheqay ye teye dong sugh xiyine'onh iy in'e
an sitl'oxiyighe'on adhitlvatr xuyił an'a dingit'anh."
"Tsoo, siqa' izoo---," yiłne.

1. Raven, the visitor, speaks in Koyukon, the language spoken by upriver people.

She went back inside and sharpened her poor little ulu.
Then she started skinning [the animal].
E---y, how it was!
It was a black bear.
How fat it was!
In the fall it had really fattened itself up.
Somehow, she managed to skin it.
She hung the skin up behind the cache.
She cut it all up; how thick its fat was!
She sliced off some of the fat and the meat,
cut pieces into the pot, and started boiling it, the poor, dear thing.
She had had only dried fish and fresh fish to eat before that.
She started boiling it, and when it had boiled, she started eating.
She stored the meat in the ground in her pit cache.
She soon had it all stored away nicely.
When she had it nicely stored away, she gathered dried willow wood.
She started to live very well on that [meat].
She had never had fat to eat before, and now she started eating good fat.
Once in a while she made ice cream for herself too, and she lived very well.
All this time, she had an awl with her, the awl that she used.
Hmm.
She was living there and the weather turned cold.
When it had turned cold, all of a sudden she heard someone at the door.
Someone was walking up to the door.
Someone came to the door and started cleaning his boots.
After a while, a skinny man came in,
a man with a dark face.
"Grandma!
Cold, cold, cold! Grandma! Cold, cold, cold!" he said to her.
"Someone is here, it seems.
Go on, sit across [the room] there," she told him.
He went across the room.
Meanwhile, the pot was boiling by the fire.
She took it off [the fire].
She put it up beside herself and ladled out some of the food.
She gave him some food in a little dish.
"Grandma," he said, "how did you ever catch this [bear]?" he said.
"Last fall my grandchildren brought it to me before freeze-up, and
what they gave me, I cooked, and just now you came."
"Granny, my feet are co---ld," he told her.

"Siqa' izoo--- nilaanh," yiłne.
"Gila ixudiniy, ngiqa' ningłgging' ts'in' ntedoyh.
Che ndadz datane' ts'i'at?" yiłne.
Yit xizro lo che enadhoł di.
"Itsoo," yiłne, "ngoxo tritr ditatl-'eł.
Tseg ngoxo ditatl-'eł.
Ts'in go dist'anh," yiłne.
"Ngo sighu tritr ditr'ił'anh ts'i xiq'adi'ist'i' ts'in', se xaxa ndadz dhist'a?
Ts'i'at sighu tritr diteł'eł?" yiłne.
Axaxiłdi venhdida' tritr oqo tadhiyo
yitongo yixudz yik'o'.
"E---y, che diva tlagg sighu neyoninh?
Ngo viq'adi'ist'i' ts'in' anh," inedhinh.
"Ngo sigixatoheł hitlagg gaq'a ngichogh ihonh anh," ne ts'ixuyił.
Nginigg tritr oqo tadhiyo xuyił q'iy tritr tlagg xuyił tr'andilighux.
Nnn.
"Natsoo, Natsoo," yiłne.
"Gitl'iq'at ło got," vazrne.
"Ngo vav idiniso hiłtiy.
Gan chux ngihonh ts'i'at," datane' yiłne.
"Q'agh ntedoyh ndadz dingit'anh ts'i'at," yiłne.
Xidigał xizro lo che yixudz yatithinax di yigixatadhon'.
Yixudz yitl'oyiditrig yixudz tr'iditayh.
Yixudz ixudiniy vitr'ixudełdił.
Yixudz ndadz go ditoneł ts'in'?
Vav ixutadhinek.

Yitongo engtthegh xiłdi engthi ngidot
totthidl xuchux dixide'o.
Xidigał yixudz *she want to get rid of him.*
Dingt'a, "Ndadz xaxa doghotlaghinh?" inedhinh:
"Gaq'a ngitthe' ngitthe' ggusr yan' ts'i'at?" yiłne.
"Sitthe' oggusr,
sitthe' ningiłtrił gila, tsook'aał," vazrne.
"Tsook'aał," vazrne.
"Ey'," yiłne.
"Ngo ngitthintatltrił," yiłne.
Yitthintitltrił yitots'in'.
Yitongo go dit'ox xiyeyighetonh yiggi diggi'etthiy.
"Go ngitthe' sitth'in q'idz ditthidhili'onh," yiłne.
Yitth'in q'idz ditthiyighidhi'onh.
Yitthintitltrił yiggiy diggi'etthiy yidzeghiłtits.

"My feet are co---ld," he told her.
"Well then, warm up your feet and leave.
Why are you saying that, anyway?" she asked him.
He spent the night there.
"Grandma," he said, "I'll get wood for you.
I'll get wood for you.
I'll do this," he said.
"Well, I don't want anybody to fetch wood for me; can't I do it myself?
Are you going to fetch wood for me?" she said.
The next morning he went after wood,
even though she didn't want him there.
"Hey, who's this no-good bum who came to me?
I don't want him," she thought.
"He'll eat up all my food; that no-good bum eats too much," she said.
He went after wood; then he came back hauling some rotten, old willow wood.
Hmm.
"Grandma, Grandma," he said.
"I'm hungry now," he said to her.
"Well, I don't have any food.
You eat so much, anyway," she started telling him.
"Go back to where you came from; what are you doing here, anyway?" she asked him.
Finally, though, she got tired of him and they started eating.
She just gave him food and whatever she had.
He just gobbled it right down.
What was she to do?
The dried fish was starting to run out.

Well, at this time, out in the river on the ice,
there was a big, open hole.
Finally she want[ed] to get rid of him.
Thinking, "How can I get rid of him?" she did the following:
"Why is your head, why is your head so dirty, anyway?" she said to him.
"My head is dirty.
Come and wash my head for me, old woman," he told her.
"Old woman," he called her.
"Sure," she told him.
"I'll wash your head," she told him.
She started washing his head right away.
She had concealed that awl behind her.
"Put your head here on my lap," she told him.
He put his head on her lap.
When she started washing his head, she stuck that awl in his ear.

"Enga!" tr'in'ne ts'in' yixudz tth'itr'ithitthiyh yił
yitoyigg yixudz ayiggi diggizriłdhiy dhi'onh.
Iy itlyił yixudz iy axa yizrik ghetthit yixudz.
"E---y che diva tlagg danh che diva got sivav gixatadhon'!" yiłne
Yixudz yighetthit ts'in' yixudz
ngitthing yixudz vith t'ogh yixudz xit'iyighiłghith anh.

Ts'an yitots'in' xałts'in' xałts'in' nigitithdon'.
Ixuxuyił xizro lo che ngi'o xido q'utr'itiht'ots di.
Gah!
Yiggi diva xizro lo che yiggi dran yidhitłghaninh tlagg.
Xizro lo chenh xidonghidoł xizro lo chenh.
"Nitsoo! Zruh zruh zruh!"
"E---y! yiłne.
"Gan gide che tr'ot'igh dingit'a sik'o' t'o' dhedo sigixatahon',"
yiłne.
"Ngo ngighu tseg ditatl-'eł ago dist'anh," vazrne ło go.
"Dalik'ał ts'in' nongidoł, ngo ngiq'adi'ist'i ts'in'," yiłne.
Venhdida' che
"Sitthe' che getiy dingt'a," vazrne.
"Sitthe' yixudz ggusr yan' gil sitthe' che tingi'ox,"
vazrne.
Yiggi diggi'etthiy che deg xiyenyighetonh che
yitthintitltrił xuyił yidzegighiłtits chenh.
Axaxiłdik
go yilogging go yilogging ndadz xiq'i yilogging go xughoy yinatht'ith.
Axaxiłdik go yighu ginetthiyh diggi'etthiy axa.
Ngi'o hiłdik tso k'idz didh'onh vighu doghyighide'onh.
He---y.
Yitots'in' ndadz go diyitoleł ts'in'?
Ixuxuyił engthi ngido' totthidl xichux dixide'onh.
"Yit engthi ngido' go hits'in' xitlagg itidhitlgholinh anh," inedhinh.
Yit yixudz engthi ngido' niłk'oyineggisr.
Yixudz totthidl yixudz xitl'ot in'at tiyidighiłtsitl.
Engthi ngido' viyił xit'ox ntighałtthit.
Yit viyił xit'ox nitighałtthit.
De---.
Yeg yixudz yeg ixuxuyił in'a han diyidenig ts'in' ło got.
Yixudz yitots'in' yixudz getiy sidałts'eyh.
I---y sidałts'eyh ghiluq.
"Agidet! Vitthoghixidhis'onh!" yinedhinh.
Yitongo *meat* yił yixudz yiq'an-gadehon' yixudz.

"Ow!" he cried, and he stretched out, and
above her there was a wooden mallet.
She grabbed it and with it she pounded his body all to pieces.
"Hey, who's this no-good bum who started eating all my food!" she said.
She pounded him all over,
and then she dragged him down [to the river] and threw him right over the bank.

Then in the evening she was starting to eat her supper.
Suddenly, somebody was walking around out by the door.
Ugh!
Who was it, but that no-good bum she had killed that day.
He just walked right back in.
"Grandma! Cold, cold, cold!"
"Hey!" she said.
"Why don't you stay away from me, you bum. You're eating all my food,"
she said to him.
"Why, I'm doing this to get firewood for you," he said.
"Shut up and get out of here. I don't want you," she told him.
The next morning,
"My head is really bad again," he said to her.
"My head's just nothing but dirt. Come and wash my head again,"
he said to her.
She kept that awl behind her again, and once more, as soon as she
started washing his head, she stuck it in his ear again.
And then
she cut off his claws, up to here [gesturing].
She poked a hole through them with her awl.
Then she hung them up on her little cache.
He---y.
What could she do with him now?
There was that big hole in the ice, out in the middle of the river.
"I should throw him into that hole out there," she thought.
She dragged him out there.
She threw him into the open hole.
Down there the rushing water pulled him under the ice.
The rushing water pulled him under the ice.
O---h.
After that, she never heard from him again.
She was just really happy.
I---y she was happy, poor dear.
"That's it! I've gotten rid of him!" she thought.
All this time, though, he had been eating up the meat.

Yixudz iy yini'eyh ts'ixuyił tritr nitihoyh hingo
hingo tso yet yighu di'iliggoyh ts'in' yixudz yini'eyh.
Ts'ixuyił imik'i yixudz vixudidinek.

Deg yixudz xiy dixodhił xuyił xizro lo chenh.
Teqa xutl xizro lo chenh ghidił di.
Sraqay yixudz dighondinithiggit xiy,
Sraqay zring yozr viye ditl'itth'e xiy.
Dze---!
Xidixinedatl.
"Tsook'aał," xałne.
"Ayh!" ne.
"Go xiyts'in' dong dina dinaqing' gidegh tadhiyonh oyninh vintr'elnig ts'in'.
Ts'an got dixit'anh," xałne.
"Hey ngo dina'idhitltthag ts'in'.
Dina'itltthayh ts'ixe'at deg dhisdo sideyan',
an'at go siyił gitidał ts'in'
deg dhisdo, che diva anh dividuxnenh?" yiłne.
Yitongo sraqay tthanxitithidił ngi'egh xuyił go q'oxitidił.
Ixuxuyił xizro lo chenh giłigginh xidon'iliggok di.
"Eyna," yiłne,
"ay'ot tso doghdhi'onh iyiq'i eta, eta logging doghde'onh," yiłne.

I---y xutitlnek tthidixutadhit.
Ngi'in yixudz yix xuk'idz yixudz xidighałdingh.
Ts'ixuyił go tr'an sughiluq ło getiy ngitl'itth.
Ngi'in xidigał tthixititl'inek di.
Ngi'egh xiłdik yixudz tthidixitadhit.
"Ndadz dengilogginh?
Do'engiloq ey dinaqing'?"
Xuyił yixudz tthidixi'oyh.
Ngitthing xizro lo chenh tthixatitl'inek.
Two womans but the old lady getiy ło go ngitl'itth.
Ngitthing tthixatitl'inek ts'in' xidigał xizro lo chenh
engthi totthidl xits'i xititl'inek di.
Totthidl xits'i nihołnik xuyił
ayiggiy, "Totthidl tingasriłghuł," xałne.
Go tr'an sughiluq go dixin'ne.
Yixudz engtthegh yitots'in' dixiyeloq.
Deg ngitthing totthidl, ixuxuyił yiggi tr'an sughiluq
yigginh niq'ołonh ixuyił yixudz engthi tiyidighiłtsitl.
De' xiday go niq'ołonh giłigginh viyił diyit'an ts'i'enen

He was just stealing it from her; whenever she went out for wood,
he would run to the cache and steal it.
It was almost entirely used up.

Winter was passing, then something happened.
Two sleds came along.
They were full of children.
Little black children were sitting in the sleds [accompanied by two women].
Oh my!
[The women] came into the house.
"Old woman," they said.
"Yes!" she said.
"Last fall our husband went somewhere and we never heard from him again.
So we've come here," they said.
"Why, no, I haven't seen anybody.
How could I ever see anybody? I just stay here by myself
and nobody comes to me;
I just stay here. Who are you talking about?" she said.
Meanwhile, the children had gone outside and were walking around.
Then, all of a sudden, one of them came running inside.
"Mom," he said to her,
"our daddy's claws are hanging out on the cache," he told her.

I---y they jumped up and started fighting with [the old woman].
The little house was shaking.
But the little old woman was very strong.
Finally they came out of the house, fighting all the way.
They kept on fighting outside.
"What did you do to him?
What did you do with our husband?"
They were fighting all the time.
They were fighting their way down the bank.
[There were] two [women], but the old lady was very strong.
They fought all the way down the bank, and finally they fought
out toward the open hole in the ice.
As the open hole got nearer,
they said, "We'll throw you into the water hole."
They said this to the little old woman.
They kept on going toward the open hole.
Just as they got to the water hole, the little old woman
threw one woman right into it.
Oh, one woman was helping the other,

ałoche vi'oqay notin go.
Ayiggi giłigginh yixudz niyitl'iyił yixudz
Axaxiłdi yixudz yeg getiy ło go ngitl'itth go tr'an sughiluq.
Yitlyił ts'in' yixudz engthi che tiyidighiłtsitl.
Sraqay yitongo yixezreł.
Axaxiłdi diqon'ithiyo.
"I---y sraqay tlaggiy.
Gila'iy xutl giłiggi yen'uxdidał," xiłne.
Xutl yenxididatl yixudz xutl yenxixighelo yixudz tthixatitlghux.
Engthi yixudz yicheghiłtrit.
Totthidl xiviyił tontthi'ełtthit.
Yitotl'ot chenh diqon'ithiyo ts'in'
iyiggi giłiggi xutl che che sraqay yiyendinigheggit ts'in'
che che tthanyidilghux ts'in'
yit yicheghiłtrit chenh.
De', yixudz xixideghonh.
Axaxiłdi diqon'ithiyo.
"Iy che diva ntlagg ye go disititl-'an,
deg che gitr'oditlt'a ts'in' dhisdo di," inedhinh.
Ts'an ghiluq yix dhido
gho yiggiy nelang yixudz yixidonik che yixudz iy yixudine'enh ts'ixuyił
tritr hotidoyh hingo yixudz yivava' ixudiditsetl
Yuxgitsiy tlagg lo che.
Yitots'in' vav xidenek ts'in' niyughu dong adinh.
Yitots'in' tthik'oneyo dughedełtanh.
Ts'an yił niłtixunili'on' dit.

for they were two of his wives.
She grabbed the other one then.
The old woman was very strong.
Grabbing her, she just threw her into the water hole too.
The children, meanwhile, were screaming.
She went back up the bank.
"I---y, you no-good kids.
Go on, get into one sled," she told them.
They got into a sled. She put them in the sled and hauled them away.
She pushed them out onto the ice.
The current in the water hole dragged them [under the ice].
After that she went up [the bank] again and
the other sled she stuffed with the other kids, and
she dragged it down the bank, too, and just
pushed it in.
Oh, she killed them all.
Then she went back up.
"Iy, who are all these no-good people
who bother me when I'm living here in poverty?" she thought.
So she stayed there in her poor old house,
where she was running out of meat again, for he had stolen it all;
whenever she had gone for wood he had stolen all her food,
that no-good Raven.
Then her food ran out and she was without [food] for a long time.
And then she went out into the woods and hanged herself.
That is all.

The Old Lady Who Lived Alone

This old lady was living [alone] all the time and she done good. She get fish and everything, and in the fall time she get some berries and everything. She does all her work and she had little igloo house.

She was staying there and pretty soon after freeze-up she hear big noise. And I don't know for what—she start to boil hot water in her pot, just boi---ling. She was thinking to put fish in there, but she just boil that fish, just clear water, and all at once she hear noise. My, her house just shook and there was bi---g black bear coming in through the door. Grow---ling and wide, his mouth was wide open. He tell this old lady, "jump in my throat!" And the old lady said, "Leave it wide open. I'll jump in there and I'll be your supper. [Mean]while she was looking for her Indian knife, but she know she couldn't do nothing with that Indian knife.

All at once it come to her mind, "I'm going to throw that boiling water in its throat." And then, "Leave it wide open. I'll jump inside your throat. Make it real wide." And he just make his mouth real wide and she just dumped that hot water right on him. [He] just went out; he couldn't even make growl no more, and she couldn't even go out that evening, she was so scared. She was just trembling and everything. "Maybe it's out there waiting for me," she was thinking. All kinds of things she was thinking.

Next morning in the morning she woke up. There was near her cache bi---g bear was stretch[ed] out. She got a long stick and she poked it. And it was stiff. So she club it and it never move. She went to it and she touch it and it was just died, just not very long ago. She went in the house and she got her Indian knife and she skin it. She have hard time to skin it, it was so big. She cut it up. She put it in the cache save. The fat was this fat because in the fall time they get so fat. She just save the guts and everything and she just save everything from it. She put [it] in her cache, and she had little [place] where she keeps some fish eggs and things, like little igloo and under the ground. She put some more, some of the meat in there too. Gee, she start to live good. Once in a while she just cook fat and meat and she eat dry fish with it, and "My---," she was saying. "How wonderful! How in the world I got that one?" she was thinking to herself.

All at once in the fall time, somebody was at the door. It was little man coming in. "My grandmother! I'm cold, I'm cold!" he said. "Well," she say, "I don't want nobody in here. I don't want you. You go back where you come from. I'm going to give you a little lunch, and then you'll go. Because I don't want nobody. I never had nobody with me all my life and I don't want nobody to camp with me," she said. "Oh, my feet is too cold," he said. "I'm just cold." "Well, how you came, you can go back. I'll just feed you and you go back." No, he don't want to go back. He want to camp with her. "How you got this meat, grandmother?" he said. (He talk the [up]river [language].)

[Part of story missing: She told him her grandchildren had given her the meat. He told her he would stay and collect wood for her, but she didn't want him to stay. He said his head was dirty and asked her to clean it for him. She agreed, and while she was cleaning it, she poked him with her awl. She took his body away, but he came back the next day.]

"*I---y gan,* why you come back again? I don't want you back. You eat all my food, and I'm not even going to live through the winter now. I'm going to just starve on account of you. I had lots of food and you been stealing from me while I go for wood. You shouldn't come around," [she] say.

"Well, I want you to wash my head again tomorrow, 'cause my head is still itchy and it's dirty," he says. So she tell him, "Okay." And she got that poker again. She poke in his ear and she just club [him] and just tore him all up. And then there was, on the ice where it's not froze, big current in there. It's not froze; it's open place. She kill him and she drag him out there and she just throw him in the water and down it went. Now she got rid of him. But, she cut his finger about this much, right there to the joint, this little finger. She poke hole in it and then she hang it on her cache hanging down. I don't know what she did that way.

And about one week after that, all at once two sleds came to her place. They tell her, "We lost our husband since this fall. Our husband start to hunt and never come back. You see our husband?" And she say, "No, I don't see nobody. I'm a lone old lady and I never see nobody." It made her mind that was their husband she killed. And those little girls, they go out and start to play around, and pretty soon one little girl came in.

"Mom," [she] say, "our daddy's small finger is hanging on her cache." My! "What you do to him?" they say, and they start to fight with her. But the little house was all upset. They just couldn't get her down—she's too powerful. Then they went outdoors and they start to go over the bank. They try to throw her, but she threw them far away from each other. They come to her and fight with her, kids and all screaming. Pretty soon they went to that open place where there's big current. "We going to drown you, old woman. You kill our husband," they tell her. "That's how you kill him," they tell her. "no," she said, "I didn't kill nobody. But you can throw me in and get rid of me. You both woman, young womans, you can do that to me if you want to," she said.

They went out and all at once she grabbed this woman and she just throw her in that open place. The other woman just came and [she] throw her in that [too], and so she got rid of those two woman. Then them kids were just screaming. She put them in the sled, one whole sled. Little dark kids, dark complexion. She just throw that one sled in there. She shove it and she shove that other sled. Then she went up into her place. Then she start to cry.

"My," she said. "I been living here a good many years by myself. What kind of people is that [who] lead me in the wrong way? Now I don't have no food. Now I'm going to die myself," she say. "I don't want to live for what I done." So she went in the woods, and I don't know what she done to herself. That was the end.

Nołdith Gixudhoy
Hawk Owl Story

Nołdith Gixudhoy

Nołdith tr'in'ne yi xidentl'iyo.
Nnn, axaxiłdik xughu dingit'a ło got.
Dits'inqay nił'anh ts'in' xits'in' ntthi'it'ox ło got:
"A-a-a gila gila-a-a, ginagheyo' ggi ji,"
xiłne ło go xinł'anh hingo.
Xits'in' nigidluq ts'in' xinł'anh.
Yiggi chet giłigginh che che nił'anh.
"A gila gila— ginagheyo' ggi ggi."
Ixuxuyił ng'odz tr'o'usr ło got Yuxgitsiy.
"Isda'!" xavazrne.
"Ngo gits'i xinghodendhet," edin xavazrne.
"Ithe', 'gitth'in tisrgi' ximdene ts'i'et?" vazrne ło go.
[He's from] up the river, this Crow.
Nnn ts'in' *he don't pay no attention.*
"A gila gila— gina—' igheyo!"
go deg che, *they say.*
Nnn, *pretty soon* "Ithe' 'gimagg chux' xividene ts'i'at?" vazrne ło go.
Ngo ixuxuyił yitongo iłt'et ło go gidile go dadz din'ne ts'in'
"A gila gila— ginagheyo' ggi ji ges."
"Ganhtse ginanghidizriq xividene anh," vazrne.
Xizro lo che yits'in' ghołtl'itth di.
Yixudz tthidixitadhit yitots'in'.
Yiggi Yuxgitsiy yixudz xitr'ethtlux ło got.
"GGAQ!" didiyoq.
Che diggandi'ełtrit che tthidanxutithidhit
ayigging nołdith che che xitr'ethtlux.
"IH!" didiyoq.
Che tthidonxitithidhit che Yuxgitsiy che xantr'etht'ix.
"GGAQ!" tr'in'ne yixudz tr'inilq'ak ngidiq.
Ngo yiggiy nołdith ggoy nginiggi yixudz tthik'ogixenathtl'isr.
Ts'an ts'in' idixunil'on'.
Yuk.

Hawk Owl Story

They say that some owls were sitting up high somewhere.
[A mother hawk owl] was pleased with her children.
She nodded towards them [and sang happily]:
"A-a-a gila gila-a-a, so, so handsome ggi ji,"
she sang to them as she looked at them.
She smiled at them as she looked at them.
She looked at one of them again.
"A gila gila---so, so handsome ggi."
Suddenly, Raven came from outside.
"Friend!" he said.
"You don't speak to them the right way ," he told [her].
"Think, why don't you call them, 'big fat legs'?" he asked her.
[He's from] up the river, this Crow.[1]
[She didn't] pay [any] attention.
"A gila gila--- so handsome!"
she sang this again, they say.
Pretty soon he told her, "Think, why don't you say to them, 'big eyes'?" he asked her.
All this time she kept on singing, saying,
"A gila gila--- so handsome ggi ji ges."
"Tell them their noses are crooked," he said to her.
At that, she attacked him.
They started to fight.
She knocked Raven right down.
"CAW!" he shouted.
He jumped back up and started fighting again,
and this time he knocked the owl down too.
"IH!" she shouted.
They started fighting again and she flung Raven down again.
Saying "CAW!" he just flew away overhead.
Then the young owls all flew away into the woods.
That is all.
Yes.

1. In Deg Hit'an stories Raven sometimes speaks Koyukon, a language spoken upriver from where these stories were told.

Q'iwałdal Tixgedr Yił
Spruce Grouse and Mink

Q'ivałdal Tixgedr Yił

Nił'edaye q'ugixidałdiyh tr'itl q'avon.
Tr'itl q'avon nixitit'usr ts'in' q'ugixidałdiyh.
Q'o q'uxeteyh nił'in.
Niłghun' nigixididluq ts'ixuyił ło got.
Deg yixudz dixit'anh dran nixudidhit.
Ndadz isre' tr'ixinedhit ts'in' dixit'anh ło got.
Axaxiłdik idivenhditux yixi xiłdik tr'itl q'avon xuyozr xuyił xathtanh ts'in' viłxenathdix ło got.
Gixithon ts'in' ts'ixuyił.
Gan xitoheł?
Deg yixudz dixit'anh.
Niłghun' nigixididluq ts'ixuyił
"Se n'at getiy nedhodi gititldiyh," niłixidin'ne ts'in' ło got.
Ixuxuyił ngidugg ts'in' gixidełdik.
Xuyił ayiggi giłiggi ngichoghinh che viq'o' yixudz ndagh sre' srilti'ełdik.
Axaxiłdik xiyoqo nixutitl'iyo.
Tr'itl q'avon nixit'usr.
Nginixi xuyił nixitit'usr ts'in'.
Ndagh n'ełdik?
Deg yixudz dixit'anh.
"Anixi che nginixi che tr'ixunił'anh," niłixidin'ne.
Axaxiłdik nginuggits'in' xitidhi'ots.
Deg nginixi ngido' xo'isr xuyił xizro lo chenh.
Do'o xizro lo chenh xiyh yix xinxughe'odi xizro lo chenh.
Xinxudinditał q'idixet'a.
Axaxiłdik yit nixine'ots.
Duxsin xixudhi'ots.
Ngiyiggi xuyet tthixighetthiyh ts'in' ngiyiggi xixenitl-'an' xuyił xizro lo chenh.
Nginuggi yix nedr xizro lo chenh yixudz vanhgiq chux dhiqonhdi.
Tth'ok chux yet, ggołdi tth'ok chux yet.
Vanhgiq chux nenithitth'aq eyiggiy viq'o' vinighe'odi xizro lo chenh.
Go yigixidełdik ts'in' duxsin yalq'at xits'in' vinyediquyh ts'in' ło got.
Yiggi yixudz ngi'o xudoy xiyixiligguk xiłdi xiyixighe'ots.
Diq'o' ni'itlyił yit.
Go lo che ne'ełdik iy "Ey xiday tr'idetsan'," xin'ne lo go.
Iy vanhgiq xiyititl'it'et.

Spruce Grouse and Mink

Two cousins were shooting arrows near the edge of the willows.
They went around shooting arrows near the edge of the willows.
Each carried a bow and arrow.
They were laughing at each other, they say.
That's all they did the whole day long.
Whenever they woke up they did this.
And every day they would lie down at the edge of the willows and they would fall asleep.
They didn't eat.
What would they eat?
This was all they did.
Laughing at each other,
"I can shoot an arrow really far," they said [to each other].
And they shot one quite high.
That bigger boy shot his arrow away somewhere.
And then they searched for it.
They went around the edge of the willows.
They kept going upland.
Where did it go?
They kept looking.
"Let's look back up there," they said to one another.
And then they went upland.
They were going along back inland, [going] downstream.
And then, over there stood a winter house.
It appeared to be low and flat.
And they went to it.
They went on top of it.
They stuck their heads inside and took a look around.
There in the middle of the house was a bowl of Indian ice cream.
It was in a big bowl, a big visitor's bowl.
That arrow of his was sticking out of that Indian ice cream.
They had shot it there, and it had fallen through the window and into [the ice cream].
So they went through the doorway and entered the house.
He retrieved his arrow there.
And then the one who had shot the arrow said, "We're so hungry."
So they started licking up that ice cream.

Yixudz ngiyixi xuyił xitltanh ine' che iłt'e yixudz a getiy yixudz
xiye xidigał xizro lo chenh gixidiłt'et.
Ndadz go xitoneł ts'in' vił axa dixidiyoq.
Ts'ixuyił ło got ixuxuyił ło got engodz xizro lo chenh tthe'oł chux itltonh angodz.
Engodz ts'in' che che q'oł chux dhi'onh, noqoy.
Axaxiłdik iy ghoyix sriłtineyo yiggiy giłigginh.
Giłigginh che che tthe'oł chux ghoyix sriłtineyo.
Yit xizro xuxiniyh viłxintl'idaq ło got.
Deg ndadz isre' viłxinałtingh xuyił.
Xiviyił ngan' xiviyił didinenh xiq'idi xizro lo chenh tr'ixilighith.
"Isda," xin'ne, niłixidin'ne.
"Gan go din'ne?" xin'ne.
Gogide deg dixet'a xizro lo chenh ntr'idit'ith xiq'i ngi'odz xits'in'.
Ixuxuyił ayiggi tthe'oł ghoyix sriłtineyo.
Deg natitl'itrit xuyił xizro lo chenh diggadhi'oy k'idz itltonh.
Vitl'o ghiłqatthdi xiyenxidilighul.
Axaxiłdik giłigginh che che ngiyixi natitl'itrit.
Tthe'oł [*sic*] t'ox natitl'itrit.
Q'oł yozr che vitl'o dolningh.
Dadz dixiyełinh ts'in' xiłdi yixudz getiy ło go xinitljit.
"Isda yozr," niłixidin'ne.
"Gan sre' idit'anh? Dina lo che xelanh," xin'ne.
Axaxiłdik yit yixudz dixet'a xuyił xizro lo chenh.
Ngi'odz xizro lo chenh yixudz xiyentr'ot'isrdi iy gan xizro lo chenh!
Ngin'qo xudina' chux na chenh niłidina ghigholinh.
Giant ło go che dit'anh.
Iy yixudz nginugg vanhgiq chux yighun' xidontithiyo.
Viye xiditth'iq.
Viyet xiyegixidiłt'et ło got.
Yixudz idintr'ighiłtthil ts'in' yixudz viqitr'itlquyh yixudz.
"Diva ngiye xighiłt'et?" vazrne yiggiy go tth'ok.
Ixuxuyił yiggiy go tth'ok din'ne,
"A engodz gide tthe'oł t'ox sriłtineyo anh siye xighiłt'edinh,"
didiyoq ło go tth'ok.
Yiggi tthe'oł gidintr'inłghił di xizro lo chenh.
Doyix xizro lo chenh chel yozr yit'ox sriłtidhido di.
Tr'itlyił yixudz thagg tr'ilighił.
Yixudz vigitr'itadhinix ts'in' xizro xiday chel k'idz yozr anh.
Chel yozr go ditr'ił'anh.
Che vighun' nontr'ełtthit engthit.
"Diva ngiye xighiłt'et?" vazrne.
"A engodz gidet q'oł t'ox dhido anh siye xighiłt'et."

They just ate and while they were still lying there,
they just kept licking the ice cream.
And then, as one would expect, they became sleepy.
Across [the room] was a big pillow.
On the other side there was a big whetstone made of stone.
And then one of them hid under it.
And the other boy hid under that big pillow.
Soon they both fell asleep.
Here they slept for some time.
And then the ground shook, and suddenly they were startled.
"Friend," they said [to one another].
"What's that?" they said.
After a while someone was coming in from outside.
And one of [the boys] was hiding there under the pillow.
He felt around there and there was a little knife.
It fell into his hand and he was holding it.
And then [the other] one of them reached down.
He felt beneath the pillow [*sic*; should be whetstone].
A small whetstone fell into his hand.
Holding [these things], they became quite frightened.
"Little friend," they said to one another.
"What is that? It is a man," they said.
They were there for some time.
Then, from outside, someone was entering!
It was a big man who kills people.
It was a giant.
He went over to that big bowl of ice cream.
The inside was licked clean.
Its insides [contents] had been licked up.
Moving angrily, he kicked it.
"Who ate your insides?" he said to that bowl.
And then that bowl said,
"That guy who is hiding under the pillow ate my insides,"
that bowl said that.
Then he grabbed that pillow.
Below there that young boy was hiding under it.
[The giant] grabbed him and put him in his mouth.
Then he started to swallow him, that little boy.
He did that to that little boy.
The giant went up to [the bowl] again angrily.
"Who ate your insides?" he said.
"The one across there under the whetstone ate my insides."

Q'oł che gidin tr'idiniłtsitl.
Ixuxuyił yit xizro lo che che q'idighidhilinh che yit dhido.
Anh che thagg tr'ilighił.
Vighun' nontr'ełtthit.
"Diva ngiye xighiłt'et?" vazrne.
Giq'idiłtth'iq xizro lo chenh.
Yiy xividisresrdititl'iningh.
"Dinavit yił tr'iłcheth.
Tthidhuxłdaq," sraqay xivazrne hingo dinavit tr'iłcheth hingo.
Xividisresrdititl'iningh.
Iyiggiy diggadhi'oy k'idz tr'iyiniłtonh.
Ndadz go xaxa xiyił tr'ixixitohał ts'in'.
Yixudz ye xaxa xuyił go xighiłtr'eth ts'ixadinh.
Nigixitidhiq'onh xivivit yet ngiyiq go noqoggiy q'oł axa.
Go nixiyiq'o xuyił dinavit tr'iłcheth yitongo.
"Sraqay tlagg yit tthidhuxłdaq!
Sigivanhgiq ixiduxłt'et," xivazrne.
Yixudz ndadz got che dixitoneł ts'in'?
Gixitighołtr'ethdi qul.
Xividisresrdititl'iningh ts'ixuyił.
Ngidugg yixudz go xiyidrogg go xughoy xinyighetthiyh ngiyuxts'in' getiy ts'in'.
Yitots'in' yixudz xiyicheghiłtrit.
Yixudz ngiyugg yixudz xiyivit yixudz yił tr'ixiyighet'otth yixudz.
Tthinixethtlux yit.
Yitongo niłt'idinitl'itsit.
Xiyidhitlghanh ts'in'.
Iyiggi diq'o' ni'itlyił yixudz ngi'in tthanxiliggok.
"Iy imk'i dinagheghonh anh."
Ngi'ot ttheting nixititl'iyo xuyił.
Niłansiyhxinitltsenh.
Axaxiłdik ngitthing tr'anxititht'ots.
Ngitthegh yiggi nixixiniłghun' ts'ixuyan' di xits'in' nixititht'ots.
Ngine' nixititht'ots ixuxuyił xizro lo chenh yixudz niłghun' nigixitithidluq.
"Hey," yiłne.
"Isda," yiłne.
"Nginoxded yixudz dithiq'isr," yiłne.
"Angidedig che che nganhtse loy xuliq'uł," yiłne.
"Ngidhayix xuyił xuliq'uł," yiłne.
Niłghun' nigixitithidluq.
Ixuxuyił xizro lo chenh eyiggi vinoxded dithiq'isr vazrnenh.
Q'ivałdal ngilanh ts'in' net'uqdi hingo
eyigginh giłigginh che che tixgedr ngilanh ts'in' yixo'in ghidiquk.
Idixunili'on'.

He moved that whetstone.
And there sat the other young boy.
He swallowed that boy too.
He went up to [the bowl] angrily.
"Who ate your insides?" he said to it.
And then it became quiet.
And then they [in the giant's stomach] began to suffocate.
"Someone is hitting my stomach.
You keep still," he told the children as they hit his stomach.
They were beginning to suffocate.
One of them brought out the little knife.
There was no way they could talk.
They could barely breathe.
Inside the stomach they started to sharpen [the knife] with a whetstone.
While sharpening it, they struck the stomach.
"You lousy kids, keep still!
You ate all my ice cream," [the giant] told them.
What were they going to do?
They couldn't breathe.
And they were about to suffocate.
They thrust the point up against the inside of his chest.
They pushed it against him.
Then they cut out his entire stomach.
They jumped back out of there.
Meanwhile, he fell over.
They had killed him.
That boy grabbed his arrow back and they [both] ran outside.
"Iy, he almost killed us."
And they stood outside.
They were catching their breath.
And then they came out by the shore.
They were playing again as they went.
And then they went upriver, and again they laughed together.
"Hey," one said.
"Friend," he said to the other.
"Your eyelid is all red," he said to him.
"And you, the end of your nose is white," the other said.
"And it is white under your chin," he said to him.
They laughed at each other.
And that is how that [spruce grouse] came to have red eyelids, they say.
Being a spruce grouse, it flew away, while
the other one, being a mink, ran away.
That is the end of it.

Spruce Grouse and Mink

Two little boys was playing bow and arrow along the edge of the willow. They play around and just play, laughing. Two cousins. And they were just walking around. They don't know where they came from. They were just playing in there. All at once, one of the little boy[s], he just don't know where his arrow went. And they start to hunt back and forth, back and forth. They look around in the woods. And they went farther back. And they were going down again. And all at once, the little bigger cousin say, "Here's an igloo. Let's go on top and we'll look inside. Maybe [we'll find] what became of that arrow." They went on top of it. They look down. Gee, there was a big dish of ice cream, about this big a dish. And the arrow was just smack right in the middle of that ice cream. "Look at that! My arrow! We'll go in there."

They went in there and they took [the arrow] out. "Let's eat [the ice cream]. We're so hungry. My, that's nice ice cream," they say. There was a big pillow on that side. Big stone over there. Sharpening stone. Big blanket in there. They went to it. Their stomachs were just big around. They finish [eating] inside. "I'm gonna hide under that pillow, one side. And you hide under that stone." And under that stone there was a little knife under there, under that stone. So [he] got that little [knife]. Under the pillow there was a little sharpening stone. Under that stone was a little knife, and under that pillow was a little stone. They had [them] in their hands. They fall asleep. They never eat before, and they just fell asleep.

And pretty soon they hear thump, thump, thump! They woke up. A big noise was coming. Just like somebody walking. My! All at once [it] came in. Big giant come in! He just went to that dish and kick it. "Who eat the ice cream?" He saw that dish. "He's under that pillow hiding, the one that eat me up," that plate say. [The giant] grabbed that pillow and there was a little boy. He just grabbed that little boy and just swallow[ed] him. "And another one, under the stone. There's one more over there," [the dish said.] And he just grab that one and swallow that boy too. He just went in and just kick it again. "Anybody else?" [the giant asked the dish.] "No, only two little boys that eat me up. All the ice cream was in me," that dish say.

And [the giant's] stomach was just moving around. And [the boys] just box [punch] his stomach [from inside]. "You kids keep still. You eat all my lunch, all my ice cream. Now you are my food." And they didn't know what to do. They just sharpen that little knife. Inside they were just boxing his stomach, and they couldn't breathe, just like they were gonna die. They gonna smother any minute. And they just sharp[en] that little knife and they poke it right through and they open [his stomach] and they jump right out. And the giant just fell over dead. They were just happy and laughing. And they jump out and the just ran out. "My! We kill that giant!" they say, and they just ran out.

They went in the willow, and they would start to walk up there with their arrow. And this one little boy, he look at [the other]. "My little cousin," he say, "my, your eyebrows inside is just red." And the other one, he said, "Your nose, under your chin, it's white. You look so funny now." They were just laughing about each other, walking up. And all at once the one with red on its eyebrow, eyelid, just flew up. A grouse! The other one just went away, that mink.

That's the end of it.

Tr'an Sughiluq Chighiligguy Gho'in Xididhitl'ighanh

The Old Woman Who Killed Herself Because of the Fox

Tr'an Sughiluq Chighiligguy Gho'in Xididhitl'ighanh

Tr'an sughiluq tr'in'ne ni'idhidhit.
Ts'an yixi dhido.
Xałts'in' tux te yił xon'idoyh ts'in' te diqon'alyayh.
Axaxiłdik nonxi'oyh tux hiłdik ditthe' yił n'iłtrił,
xiyetr'anxidałtayh; xididits'ił iłt'et.
Diyix xuyił xididits'ił ło got.
Ts'an yixudz dit'anh.
Xuyił sanhtux hiłdi ngitthegh xiłdik łegg, łegg dił'anh ixutiy ghiluq.
Xiyts'in'tux che che digathtl'enh ts'in' noghiniy ghun'.
Ixutiy yił axa xełedz xiłdi dhido.
Yix xiyozr dhido.
Nda xineg xits'il yixudz getiy ło got.
Xełedz dixidili'anh.

Axaxiłdi dithitinh.
Ditithitinh engtthegh tinh yititldaq.
Yiłdax.
Te xon'idoyh yitongo srixno' ło go dhido.
Ts'an yixudz dit'anh deg yixudz dingt'a xuyił niyinetonh di.
Łetsing yixudz xethdlat yit srixno'.
Axaxiłdik che te xontithiyo ixuyił ło go go do'o xuts'in' xizro chenh.
"Itsa'a!" vazrne di.
Yixi gidenitlningh do'ot xizro lo chenh chighiligguy q'u'edoyh di.
Chighiligguy q'uł zro lo chenh, yixudz gilegiq xiq'iy.
"Siyił gitiłghoł gila'.
Ngo ngits'id tatlał di.
Ngo getiy ngits'id gits'i dingt'a.
Siyił gitiłghoł!
Sighun' tthitełch'ił ngits'id tatlał di," yiłne.
Yitoyigg digite' yixudz ngiyix niyigheqonh
yixudz ngi'egh q'utithitrit.
Ngi'egh xizro lo chenh
dadz dighilingidh tritr yozr iłchet ey, ey axa yixudz yenitlghoł.
Yiniłghoł yixudz.

The Old Woman Who Killed Herself Because of the Fox

A dear old woman, they say, lived somewhere.
She lived there.
And in the evening she always carried up water for herself.
Every day she washed her head,
she took a bath; she kept herself clean all the time.
She always kept her house clean too.
She always did all this.
The poor dear fished in the summertime down by the river.
In the fall she always set snares for rabbits.
By these methods, she lived well.
She lived in a little house.
How nice and clean it all was.
She kept it very nice.

Then it froze up.
It started to freeze up; out on the water the ice started running.
The ice was running.
She kept fetching water while she was living by the creek.
She was doing all this, just doing everything, and then the ice stopped running.
There was ice sticking up all over on that creek.
She was fetching water again when suddenly something was right behind her.
"Grandmother!" somebody said.
She looked around there, and there was a fox walking around.
It was a white fox, pure white, like paper.
"Club me; go ahead.
I want to be your blanket.
Your blanket is really no good.
Club me!
You can skin me and I'll be your blanket," it told her.
Right away she set down the water
and hurried around there.
Right there on the ground
she grabbed a little stick about this long and tried to club it with it.
She tried to club it.

Vik'odz q'uyethtl'eth.
Go yixudz yitiłghuł xuyił che gidegh che ntiligguyh yiq'atl'ot xizro.
Yighun' xił ghotitl'itl'itth de---g yixudz ye xighun' enitlni.
Go imik'i yitlghuł
yixudz gits'idz che idiyił ntiditrik ts'in'
ngi'in che chenh vandelzim'.
Xidigał xizro lo chenh yixudz yighun' nigitathdluq di.
"Ngits'id tatlał disingilax," yiłne ts'in'.
Ixuyił ngiyix viqigitl'el diqighidiniq.
Kula!
Yixudz diqigitl'el yił don'iłchidh ts'in' yixudz
engan yixudz srixno' engan xizro lo chenh
ginet'uq xiq'i didiyoq di iyiggiy chighiligguy.
Engan yixudz yiq'i
ngo ngitthet xits'in' yixudz ngidugg vith q'idz yixudz xitl'itlux iyiggiy chighiligguy.
Iyiggi tr'an sughiluq che che yixudz ng'o yit
xits'i yixudz yinełtthit ngidugg che xitl'itlux.
Nginigg yixudz tthik'o yixudz yik'odz ngiłigidinghdi
xizro ngiyix yitongo viqigitl'el diqighidiniq.
Nginigg yixudz yiq'i nginigg xizro lo chenh
ndadz xizro lo chenh yixudz didlang chux denithitik.
Eyiłdi yixudz eyiq'idz ditl'itlux yidotith ghałtlux go chighiligguy go dit'anh.
I-i-y, iyiggi tr'an sughiluq che yixudz yił yinełtlux che idedig,
"Vitatlax yan'," inedhinh ts'in'!"
Ixuxuyił xizro lo chenh ngiyix viqa' viqigitl'el
yixudz gitthe' yixudz q'idinthitth'ix.
Yoyeghidit'iq.
Ngiyix gitthe' chux dadz dingit'ay yixudz vighu'ełtits di.
Ngiyix yixudz vidil axa yixudz xidithiq'isr.
Yit yixudz nighetlaq hingo
ngiyiggi dił dalzresr hingo ng'egh edi yixudz dił yan' axa imedz dixet'a.
Iyiggiy chighiligguy yighun' nigitathdluq.
"Xiday ngits'id tatlał di?
Ngidisne, 'Sidhiłgha',' ngidisne
ngidenagh xididhalighanh,"
yiłne ts'in' ngiyix yixudz yidil yet q'utithighith.
Yidil yet q'u'idighith.
Xudigał xizro lo che yixudz didiq'asr di
q'odet deg vivid xizro lo chenh vivid tr'alts'in' xiliq'uł xiyozr.
Hingo nginet vicha' che che
go *this long* vicha' chet hiliq'uł.

It was running away from her.
She kept hitting at it and it ran away again; there it was behind her.
In the darkness of night a---ll over the place, she got very tired.
She would almost hit it
and it would just run back around the other side, and
zip by her again and again.
Then it finally started laughing at her.
"I'll be your blanket—kill me," it was telling her.
Her bootlace was untied.
Poor thing!
She didn't even tie up her bootlace, and
right across that creek
the fox went, just as if it were flying.
She went across after it,
and the fox leaped from the shore up onto the cutbank.
The dear old woman went after it there;
she charged after it up the bank where it had jumped.
It went back into the woods, keeping away from her,
while below her bootlace was untied.
[She went] back into the woods after it,
where there was a big spruce tree that had fallen over.
The fox leaped up onto it and jumped over it.
I-i-y, the dear old woman also jumped it herself,
thinking, "Now I'll catch it!"
But down below, her bootlace
got all tangled up in the limbs.
She tripped and fell.
She was impaled on a big limb.
Under the tree, [the ground] was red with her blood all around.
While she hung there,
below her the blood poured down until all the ground around was completely
covered with blood.
The fox started to laugh at her.
"How could I be your blanket?
When I told you, 'Kill me,' I was really
telling you to kill yourself instead,"
it said to her as it started rolling around in her blood.
It was rolling around below in her blood.
Finally it turned red,
except for a little white on its stomach.
And the very tip of its tail, too—
a place about this long on its tail-tip was white.

Hingo yixudz dił yet xidołtanh.
"Go dadz hiq'at an'at tr'an sughiluq
dadz diselax vidighixne'.
Getiy yixudz gits'idist'a.
Yixudz sidag yixudz tiliq'uł sidag dithiq'isr ts'ixiq'at an'at vidighisne',"
ne ło got.
Ts'an yitots'in' dixunili'on'.
Yuk.

All this time it just lay there in the blood.
"The dear old woman
has done for me just what I wanted her to do, just what I told her to do.
I'm just completely changed into something else.
My coat was all white, and I wanted a red coat, so I told her that,"
it said then.
That is all.
Yes.